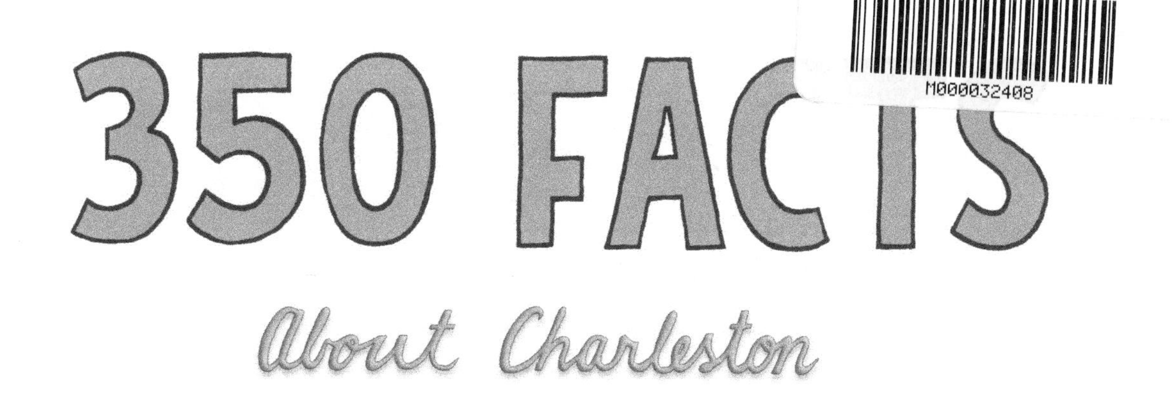

350 FACTS About Charleston

BY ANDY BRACK AND THE STAFF OF THE CHARLESTON CITY PAPER

CHARLESTON CITY PAPER

ISBN: 978-1-952248-05-4

Cover art and interior cartoons by Robert Ariail
Cover and interior design by Vally M. Sharpe

Published by
City Paper Press
an imprint of
United Writers Press
Asheville, N.C. 28803

Table of Contents

Introduction

Imagine living in Charleston 350 years ago. No air-conditioning. No bug spray. No smart phones. No grocery stores. No cars. It would have been a tough, hard life inflicted by pests, storms, turmoil, and cloying heat and humidity. Just go outside any July morning and don't go back into comfort for 24 hours. You'll quickly find out how it was. (An easier, less sweaty way to get the experience is to visit Charles Towne Landing State Park for a couple of hours.)

Despite all of the factors stacked against them, settlers, along with enslaved Africans, came and chopped trees, made forts, planted fields, explored and fanned out to discover lush riches in the New World. The Carolinas colony, started as a business venture, experienced success when landholders figured out they could grow rice and indigo. By the time 100 years passed, Charleston had become rich – a leading colonial city of its time with a long list of colonial firsts–from the first library and first fire insurance company to the first performances of theatre and opera.

This book of facts, one to honor each year of the Holy City's history, is an amalgamation of hundreds of hours of work by the staff of the *Charleston City Paper.* It brings together lots of information from different sources as snapshots of how Charleston has grown through the years. The first part of the book focuses on Charleston firsts, early settlers and two wars that put Charleston in the history books – the Revolutionary, where patriots scored a critical naval victory over the British in June 1776 – and the Civil, which started with shots fired at Fort Sumter in April 1861. What follows are chapters with Charleston facts on art, culture, education, economics, food, attractions, people and the hard road to civil rights. Some of the information may seem familiar. And some may lead you to think more than once, "I didn't know that."

If you want to do more reading, there's a selected bibliography at the end of the book. If you want to find specific sources, visit the book's website, CharlestonFacts.com.

None of this could have been cobbled together without the talented work of staffers at the *City Paper.* Lift a glass to Skyler Baldwin (SB), Heath Ellison (HE), Connelly Hardaway (CH), Mary Scott Hardaway (MSH) and Lindsay Street (LS). Thank you all.

And a hearty tip of the hat to talented cartoonist Robert Ariail whose snarky drawings about Charleston's historical past will give you more than one good laugh. We appreciate his contributions. We also are thankful for the advice, editing and production skills of Vally Sharpe of Asheville's United Writers Press.

As you read *350 Facts About Charleston,* we hope you better understand the toil and trouble that settlers and enslaved Africans went through more than three centuries ago to create a community that is the number one destination in the country.

— Andy Brack, August 2020

350 FACTS

About Charleston

Charleston firsts

1

Oldest municipal college

The College of Charleston, founded 100 years after the first settlers landed in Charleston in 1670, became the nation's first municipal college in 1837 when it came under the control of the city of Charleston. Dubbed locally as "The College of Knowledge," it is the 13th oldest institution of higher education in the United States. – *AB*

2

Birthplace of Reform Judaism

Kahal Kadosh Beth Elohim, the second oldest synagogue in the United States, is widely recognized as the birthplace of Reform Judaism. Founded in 1749 by Jews attracted to Charleston for its civil and religious liberty, members built a nationally impressive Georgian home of worship by 1794. Thirty years later, the synagogue's 47 trustees sought to change the temple's liturgy to include English translation of prayers but were denied. They resigned from the congregation and organized "The Reformed Society of Israelites," whose practices and principles are a big part of today's Reform Judaism. By 1820, Charleston was home to the largest community of Jews of any American city. The congregation's Georgian worship home burned in 1838, only to be replaced two years later with a building that has been described as "one of the country's finest examples of Greek Revival architecture." – *AB*

3

First successful submarine attack

On Feb. 17, 1864, in Charleston harbor, the 25-foot-long Confederate submarine *H.L. Hunley* became the first submarine to succeed in sinking an enemy ship—the Union warship *Housatonic*. But the Hunley sank not long thereafter in what remains a mystery. The ship was discovered in 1995 and recovered in 2000. Now, researchers in a high-tech conservatory continue to unlock the submarine's mysteries and search for why it sank. The North Charleston research center offers tours to the public. A replica of the submarine is outside the Charleston Museum, the nation's first museum. – *AB*

4

America's first museum

The Charleston Museum, located at the corner of Meeting and John streets, got started in 1773 and is, according to its website, "commonly regarded" as America's first museum. Established by the Charleston Library Society as the American Revolution brewed, "its early history was characterized by association with distinguished South Carolinians and scientific figures including Charles Cotesworth Pinckney, Thomas Heyward, Jr., the Rev. John Bachman and John J. Audubon." It has a broad, respected collection that includes everything from entomology, furniture, historic textiles, natural history, Charleston silver, jewelry and much more. It's a must-see attraction. – *AB*

5

Charleston Museum has several homes through the years

While the Charleston Museum is the nation's oldest museum, it has moved around the peninsula through the years. In its early days, the collection had public viewing parties on Chalmers Street as early as 1824, later moving to the Medical College of South Carolina. When that home needed to be torn down to build Roper Hospital, the third floor of Randolph Hall at the College of Charleston served as a home for the museum until it moved in 1907 into its own building in Cannon Park. Then in 1980, the museum moved to its current location on Meeting Street. And that was good timing because a year and a half later, the old museum burned in a spectacular fire. All that remains today are four columns in Cannon Park. – *AB*

6

First citizenship school

In 1954 in the Progressive Club on Johns Island just outside of Charleston, civil rights pioneers Esau Jenkins, Bernice Robinson and Septima Clark started the nation's first "citizenship school" after attending an organizing workshop at the Highlander Folk School in Monteagle, Tenn. The school provided a place to teach Sea Island blacks in Jim Crow South Carolina how to register to vote. "That one class in the co-op became thousands of classes in churches, schools and homes," his grandson Abe Jenkins recalled years later. "In 1962, the SCLC brought in other groups that later formed the Voter Education Project (VEP). Between 1962 and 1966, VEP trained 10,000 teachers for citizenship schools, and 700,000 Black voters registered throughout the South. By 1970, another million Black voters had registered." – *AB*

7

Birthplace of American golf

Golf in America got its start in 1786 in Charleston with the formation of the South Carolina Golf Club, whose members reportedly played on a bustling rectangle of land that stretched between what we know as Charleston and Beaufain streets and bounded by Rutledge and Barre streets. The area, called Harleston Green, seemed to disappear from historical records as a golf course around 1800. But that makes sense: Around that time, homes started being built in the area. Interesting tidbit: Some 432 golf balls and 96 clubs arrived in Charleston from England in 1743 as the first known shipment of golf equipment into the colonies.

– AB

8

S.C. educator was first Black man elected statewide in U.S.

Francis Lewis Cardozo (1836-1903), born free in Charleston, founded the Avery Normal Institute in 1865. It was the first accredited secondary school for African Americans in Charleston. Today, its successor, the Avery Institute, is part of the College of Charleston. Cardozo also offered a big political first: He was elected S.C. secretary of state in 1868, becoming the first African American to hold a statewide office in the United States. He advocated for integrated public schools, which was supported by the legislature at the time. He resigned his seat to teach Latin at Howard University, but returned to South Carolina politics in 1872 and was elected state treasurer, serving until 1877 when the federal government began to remove federal troops that protected Black participation in politics and daily life. In 1878, Cardozo was appointed to the Treasury Department in Washington, D.C., later becoming principal of the Washington, D.C., Colored High School. He lived in the nation's capital until his death in 1903. – *LS*

9

First Greek female immigrant into North America

Maria Gracia Turnbull is considered by some to be the first Greek woman to settle in North America, a claim etched into her memorial stone at St. Philip's Church. The marker reads:

> "Dedicated to the final memory of
> Maria Gracia Dura Bin Turnbull
> The daughter of a Greek merchant from
> Smyrna, Asia Minor.
> The first Greek woman to settle in North America,
> who, with her husband, Dr. Andrew Turnbull,
> established the colony of New Smyrna, Florida
> on June 26, 1768
> She, her husband and children moved to
> Charleston, South Carolina May 13, 1782."

– *AB*

10

First passenger rail service

The *Best Friend of Charleston* was a steam-powered locomotive that powered the nation's first passenger rail service following an inaugural run on Dec. 25, 1830, on a six-mile route starting in Charleston. Ironically, the *Best Friend* also became another first – the first locomotive to experience a boiler explosion in an accident on June 17, 1831. Rail service continued with another locomotive with what became a 136-mile-long route to Hamburg, S.C., then the world's longest continuous railroad. A 1928 replica of the locomotive is on display at the Best Friend Train Museum, 23 Ann St., Charleston. – *AB*

11

Nation's first historic zoning district

Ever wonder why so much of old downtown Charleston is preserved? It's because the Charleston City Council established the nation's first historic zoning district on Oct. 13, 1931, when it created the "Old and Historic District" as well as a Board of Architectural Review, which continues to serve as an authority on new projects in an effort to preserve and protect historic neighborhoods. "Today, there are more than 2,000 restored old buildings, many having tiered porches called piazzas lining narrow brick alleys, cobblestone streets and walled courtyard gardens. These architectural treasures dating from the 1600s to the Civil War have been preserved and restored under the leadership of the Preservation Society of Charleston," according to a 1989 story in *The Los Angeles Times*. – *AB*

12

First fireproof building

The Fireproof Building, home today to the South Carolina Historical Society Museum, was indeed fireproof, surviving the Great Fire of 1861. The building, designed by architect Robert Mills (America's first domestically-trained architect), was built in 1827 to house county records. At the time, the two-story Greek Revival building was the most fireproof in the nation and is considered the country's first. The museum opened in 2018 after a renovation. – *AB*

13

First American theatre and opera performances

The first theatrical season in the colonies started Jan. 24, 1735, with a play (*The Orphan,* by Thomas Otway) at the Courtroom in Shepheard's Tavern on Broad Street in Charleston. Two weeks later, the fourth performance in the series became the first opera performance produced in the colonies. On Feb. 8, 1735, viewers enjoyed an 18th-century ballad opera, "Flora: or Hob in the Well." The following year, the opera was performed at the new Dock Street Theatre and reportedly returned often. In 2010, to celebrate an $18 million renovation of the theater, composer Neely Bruce of Wesleyan University mounted a production of "Flora" during Spoleto Festival USA. – *AB*

14

First paid woman artist in America

Henrietta de Beaulieu Dering Johnston (ca. 1674-1729) was the first professional woman artist in America. Born into a Huguenot family that moved to London in 1687, it is unknown how she learned to paint portraits, although they are in the style of a popular English artist of the time. She and her second husband, the Rev. Gideon Johnston, moved to Charleston in 1708 after he was appointed bishop's commissary in South Carolina by the Bishop of London. Compared to earlier works, her portraits in America "are lighter, simpler, and smaller, indicative of the preciousness of her materials, all of which had to be imported. ... Each sitter's posture is erect, with the head turned slightly toward the viewer. Typically, large oval eyes dominate the subject's face." About 40 portraits remain. The Gibbes Museum in Charleston has 10, the largest collection of her work. – *AB*

15

First building in Southeast intended as museum

The Gibbes Museum of Art on lower Meeting Street in Charleston was the first building in the Southeast to be built specifically to house a museum. The museum is home to the Carolina Art Association, organized in 1858. In 1905, a Beaux Arts building designed by architect Frank Milburn opened as the James S. Gibbes Memorial Art Gallery. A legacy from the building's namesake allowed the association to buy the property and build the museum to display art and provide instruction. The museum has a collection of more than 500 paintings with works by Charles Willson Peale, Gilbert Stuart, Henrietta Johnston and Edward Harleston, as well as more than 600 works that comprise the nation's third largest collection of miniature portraits. In December 2017, the Gibbes reopened following a two-year, $17 million renovation. Modern acquisitions include works by Jasper Johns and Jonathan Green. – *AB*

16

"America's first theatre"

The Dock Street Theatre is known as "America's first theatre." Located originally on Dock Street (now known as Queen Street) in the heart of old Charleston, the theatre's first offering on Feb. 12, 1736, was *The Recruiting Officer.* That first theatre building likely was destroyed by fire in 1740. In 1809, the site's current building was constructed as a hotel. By 1935, it was in disrepair, but a Works Project Administration renovation during the Great Depression turned it into the theatre we know today at the corner of Church and Queen streets. In addition to serving as the residence of Charleston Stage, the largest professional theatre company in South Carolina, the Dock Street Theatre hosts numerous cultural events, including popular chamber music performances during Spoleto Festival USA. – *AB*

17

First Memorial Day

Charleston Mayor John Tecklenburg and historian Damon Fordham unveiled a historical marker May 15, 2018, that recognized Charleston as having the "First Memorial Day in the United States of America." On May 1, 1865, some 10,000 formerly enslaved people, including 2,800 children, gathered on what then was the old Washington Race Course (now Hampton Park) for a mass funeral for Union soldiers who died in a prison camp there. They sang songs, marched by graves, prayed and listened to sermons on what they called "Decoration Day," but what some now say was how "former Charleston slaves started a tradition that would come to be known as Memorial Day." While pinpointing the first Memorial Day is controversial for some, many say it is fitting for this day to be a bookend for the city where the first shots of the Civil War were fired. – *AB*

18

Birthplace of fire insurance

The first fire insurance company in America was organized in February 1736 in Charleston with the formation of the Friendly Society for the Mutual Insuring of Houses Against Fire. According to an article from 1893, "John Fenwicke, Samuel Wragg and Charles Pinckney were chosen directors; John Crokat and Henry Peronneau, merchants, secretaries; Gabriel Manigault, treasurer; Gerelt Van Velesen and John Laurens, firemasters." The company, however, "ceased business some six years later after its inception, as a result of a fire involving $1,250,000 of insurance, which was a very large sum in those times." Reportedly, more than 300 buildings were destroyed in the Great Fire of 1740. – *AB*

19

City has oldest working fire station in nation

The city of Charleston's fire station at the corner of Wentworth and Meeting streets is reportedly the oldest working fire station in the nation. The city, always under threat of fire in its early days, got its first fire department through the Friendly Society insurance company in 1736. In 1819, fire service became a volunteer effort until Jan. 1, 1882, "when a paid professional fire department staffed with 103 firefighters was formed," according to the Charleston Fire Department. – *AB*

Nation's first public statue

Charleston County Judicial Center on Broad Street is the home to an 18th-century marble statue of William Pitt (1708-1778), first Earl of Chatham, that is believed to be "the nation's first public statuary, one of the grandest tributes that survives from this nation's colonial era," according to columnist Robert Behre. The statue, which has moved at least four times through the years, was one of two commissioned to honor Pitt, considered America's leading parliamentary advocate before the Revolutionary War. Charleston's Pitt statue was delivered May 31, 1770, before a companion piece made it to New York. Interestingly, a British cannonball knocked off the statue's arm in Charleston. Later, the statue's head was separated from the torso, only to be reattached. – *AB*

21

First Chamber of Commerce

America's first Chamber of Commerce reportedly was started in 1773 in Swallow's Tavern. The tavern was the successor of Shepheard's Tavern, which originally was built on Broad Street in 1705. Through the years when there were few public buildings, the tavern played an important part in colonial life, being rented for court meetings, as the home of a Masonic lodge and as the location of the first theater performances in the colonies. During Revolutionary times, the tavern hosted meetings of the Sons of Liberty, fraternal organizations and the Society of the Cincinnati. – *AB*

22

First female publisher

Elizabeth Ann Timothy took over her late husband's newspaper company and oversaw publication of the South's first newspaper, the *South Carolina Gazette,* from 1739 to 1744. That made her America's first female editor and publisher. – *AB*

23

Oldest public gardens — and first Charleston tourist destination

Magnolia Plantation, founded by the Drayton family in the 1670s, is the oldest plantation on the Ashley River. It also "has earned the distinction as the oldest public garden in the United States," according to Explore Charleston. "The Rev. John Grimké Drayton expanded the gardens in the 1840s, opening them three decades later to steamboat passengers. As a result, Magnolia also enjoys being Charleston's first tourist destination." In 2019, the attraction hosted "Lights of Magnolia," a Chinese lantern festival illuminating the gardens for the first time in its history. – *AB*

24

So much history in one place

Charleston has 42 National Historic Landmarks – more in one county than in 30 U.S. states. Among the landmarks are the William Aiken House, Miles Brewton House, College of Charleston, Drayton Hall, Fireproof Building, Dubose Heyward House, Kahal Kadosh Beth Elohim, Powder Magazine, Nathaniel Russell House, John Rutledge House and Denmark Vesey House. – *AB*

25

The nation's first public library

According to the Historic Charleston Foundation, the title of the nation's first public library can be given to a provincial library established by the General Assembly of South Carolina on Nov. 16, 1700, in Charles Towne along St. Philip Street. However, others claim the oldest public libraries to be the Darby Free Library in Pennsylvania, which has been in continuous operation since 1743, or the library in Peterborough, N.H., which opened in 1833 as the first tax-supported free public library. – *SB*

26

The Rosebud is the first children's newspaper in the country

Caroline Howard, born in 1794 in Boston, moved to Charleston in 1819 with her new husband, the Rev. Samuel Gilman, who served as a Unitarian pastor. In 1832, she began to edit a juvenile weekly paper, *The Rosebud,* which included verses, tales and novels, which were later published in volumes. Additionally, the paper published pro-slavery content, such as a instructions for young slaveholders and critical reviews of abolitionist literature. – *SB*

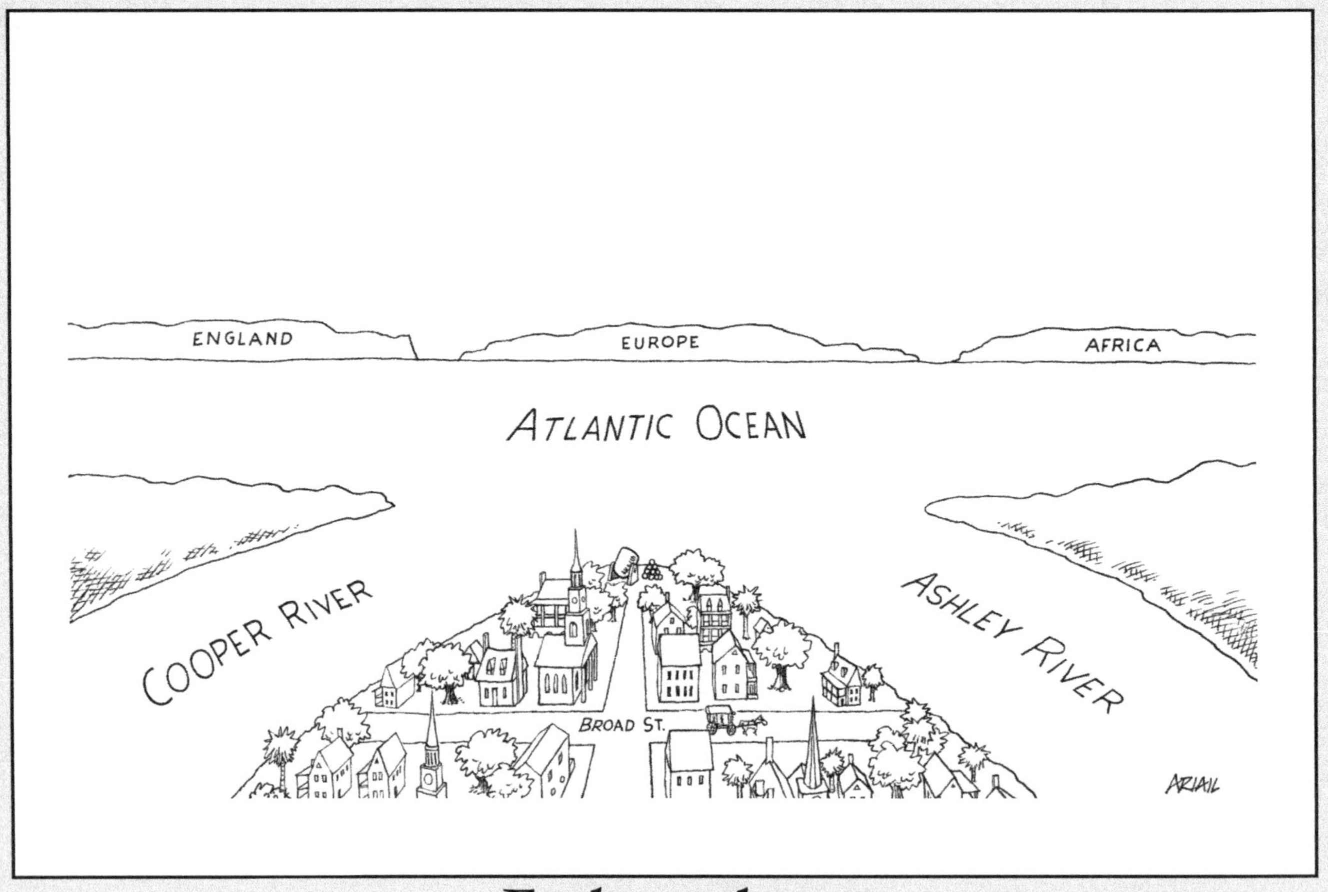

Early settlers

27

Start of the Atlantic Ocean

According to old-time wags and natives who see Charleston as the epicenter of the world, the Atlantic Ocean actually starts in Charleston harbor at the confluence of the Ashley and Cooper rivers. The late U.S. Sen. Fritz Hollings, born in the Holy City in 1922, often was heard saying, "Every great city has a great river. London has the Thames. New York has the Hudson. Washington has the Potomac. And Charleston, Andrew, Charleston has two great rivers – the Ashley and the Cooper – and that's where the Atlantic Ocean starts." – *AB*

28

Kiawah leader pointed settlers to Charleston harbor

South Carolina's Lowcountry has been inhabited by humans for more than 12,000 years, with four main tribes of Native Americans calling the landscape home – the Kiawah, Etiwan, Sewee and Coosaw. The chief of the Kiawah, known as the "Cacique," reportedly encouraged the first of the English settlers to the Charleston area and away from a settlement site at Port Royal, near Beaufort. Perhaps this is why the English settlers first called the river on which they settled on the Kiawah, rather than the Ashley. – *SB*

29

Region was occupied by natives for millennia before colonization

At least 29 distinct tribes of Native Americans lived in the borders of modern-day South Carolina before the arrival of European settlers. The names of many tribes are still with us today in places like the Stono and Ashepoo rivers, Kiawah Island and Edisto Island. The native population sharply declined after the arrival of the Europeans, who brought diseases such as smallpox and conflicts over trade practices and land. Many tribes are now extinct; a few tribes, though, still exist and are active today, including the Catawba, Pee Dee and Santee tribes. Many tribes made their homes around what would become Charleston, such as the Edisto, Kiawah, Stono and Etiwan tribes. – *SB*

30

Getting here in olden days was a nightmare for travelers

The ships that made the voyage to the Carolinas in 1669 were met with rough waters and even rougher weather. Damaged in the first trip to Barbados, ships were scattered by storms during the next outing, during which one shipwrecked and another disappeared in a hurricane. It wasn't until the following year that the expedition's surviving ship, the *Carolina,* dropped anchor at the mouth of the Ashley River, with the only known date of arrival to be "early in April," 1670. – *SB*

31

First stop: Albemarle Point

Charleston's settlers first located on the Ashley River at Albemarle Point after being directed there by the Kiawah Indian chief Cacique, who befriended the English to get guns to protect the tribe from Westos Indians near the Savannah River. "It turned out to be less healthy and less safe than first believed, and in 1680 the settlers moved across the Ashley to today's Charleston peninsula, building a palisade wall around the settlement for protection – the only English walled city in what would become the United States," historians Jack Bass and Scott Poole wrote in a 2009 history of the state. – *AB*

32

Lords proprietors started colony as business enterprise

Seven years before settlers landed in Charleston in 1670, King Charles II granted the land of the Carolinas to eight English noblemen. Between then and 1729, when King George II bought shares of the last owners, nearly 50 people claimed or owned the shares of what essentially was a business enterprise to start a colony. The original "lords proprietors" have names that are familiar along the coasts of North and South Carolina: Edward Hyde, first earl of Clarendon; George Monck, first duke of Albemarle; William Craven, first earl of Craven; Anthony Ashley Cooper, first earl of Shaftesbury; John Berkeley, first baron Berkeley of Stratton, and his brother Sir William Berkeley, governor of Virginia; Sir George Carteret; and Sir John Colleton. Ashley Cooper, namesake of the rivers marking the Charleston peninsula, persuaded other proprietors to fund the expedition that established Charleston. – *AB*

33

Locke inspired Carolina's religious liberty

Philosopher John Locke helped to draft the original *Fundamental Constitutions for Carolina* before the first settlers left England in 1670. One provision, which provided for religious liberty that reportedly exceeded anything that existed in its day in Europe, called for settlers to believe in God, which included Christians, Jews, Quakers and Huguenots. Due to the English political climate, Roman Catholics were not allowed to practice their religion freely. Despite the liberties in Locke's vision, one provision allowed for chattel slavery. None of the five drafts of the *Fundamental Constitutions* were ever accepted, but they had a great influence on how the colony developed. – *AB*

34

They just wanted the postcard

None of the original eight lords proprietors of the Carolina colony ever set foot in America. – *AB*

35

Centuries-old oak was a possible witness to the first arrivals of settlers and slaves

One particular oak on nearby John's Island can boast a significant age. The Angel Oak Tree, a Southern live oak tree inside the city limits of Charleston, is believed to be more than 500 years old or even older. Named for the ghosts of former slaves who were rumored to appear around the tree as angels, it is surrounded by a protected park to preserve its past and future. – *SB*

36

First enslaved Africans recorded by name enter region in 1670

Six weeks after the *Carolina's* arrival, a sloop called the *Three Brothers* joined the settlers. The sloop had been attacked by Indians and Spaniards on its way south from Nansemond, Virginia. Aboard the ship was the first family of enslaved Africans brought to the Carolinas to be recorded by name, John Sr., Elizabeth and John Jr. – *SB*

37

Carolina was a "colony of a colony"

Charleston and Barbados have a strong connection. In 1670, the Lords Proprietors invited Englishmen who had spent up to four decades successfully settling on the Caribbean island to be part of the expedition to start the Carolina colony. Settlers in the Carolinas imported the "Barbados Model" of governance, which included forced labor by indentured servants and enslaved Africans. "Carolina thus became what one historian called a 'colony of a colony' – a colony of Barbados," according to Rhoda Green, honorary consul for Barbados in South Carolina. Other similarities between the two are found in similar surnames, such as Drayton, Middleton and Gibbes, and similar architecture, such as how the Charleston single house may be adapted from a type of dwelling in Barbados. – *AB*

38

Slave trade boomed in early days of the colony

The only colony that had slavery from the beginning was South Carolina. Part of the first contingent of settlers arriving in Charleston were three enslaved Black people, "thus introducing into the permanent settlement the issue that would dominate much of the economic, social, and political life of South Carolina's next three hundred years." The slave trade boomed between 1720 and 1740 when an estimated 40,000 enslaved Africans came into the colony, most through Charleston. – *AB*

39

Charles Town was once the seat of power in South Carolina

Ten years after its founding in 1670 by about 200 European settlers at Albemarle Point in what is now in the West Ashley part of Charleston, the settlers and government of "Charles Town" moved across the Ashley River to the peninsula to an area formerly known as Oyster Point. Throughout the rest of the colonial period of Charleston and the American Revolution, Charleston was South Carolina's principal town and seaport, the seat of commerce and government and its most densely populated community. – *SB*

40

Charleston was heavily fortified in its early days

From the time colonists started settling the peninsula in 1680 through the Revolutionary War 100 years later, Charleston was a heavily-fortified, walled city "complete with moats, drawbridges, wooden gates with iron-strap hinges and a medieval-style wall – the better to protect against invaders and pirates," according to *Wildsam Field Guide*. Charleston's wall reportedly was the only one of its kind built in America by the British. You can still see part of the original wall in the cellar of the Old Exchange Building at the end of Broad Street. – *AB*

41

St. Philip's Church dates from 1681

The oldest religious European-American congregation in the new colony of Carolina is St. Philip's, first located at the corner of Meeting and Broad streets, which is the site today of St. Michael's Church. Construction of a wooden church started in 1680 with the congregation established the following year. When a hurricane in 1710 damaged the building, the congregation built a new church a few blocks away on Church Street. The current sophisticated building dates from 1831, though the spire was finished in 1850. A cemetery on church grounds features a who's who of prominent Charlestonians, including Col. William Rhett, who brought pirates Blackbeard and Stede Bonnet to justice; Edward Rutledge, a signer of the Declaration of Independence; Charles Pinckney, a framer of the U.S. Constitution; and John C. Calhoun, a vice president and U.S. senator. – *AB*

42

Mother church for Baptists

First Baptist Church of Charleston is considered the mother church of the Southern Baptist Convention, according to historians Jack Bass and Scott Poole. A congregation first organized in 1700 following the tradition of French theologian John Calvin, it later departed from its Reformation roots to join the Southern Baptist tradition. – *AB*

43

Old St. Andrew's Parish Church

Old St. Andrew's Parish Church is the oldest church structure south of Virginia that still hosts regular services. Located west of the Ashley River, it was one of 10 Anglican churches established in South Carolina by the Church Act of 1706, which named the Church of England the official church of the state. Among the wealthiest parishes, St. Andrew's served wealthy plantation owners along the Ashley River. The Rev. John Grimke Drayton, owner of Magnolia Plantation, was rector of St. Andrew's for 40 years in the mid-19th century, preaching to both plantation owners and the enslaved. – *CH*

44

Oldest society in the world

The St. Andrew's Society of Charleston, formed in 1729 by several local Scots in honor of Scotland's patron saint, is said to be the oldest St. Andrew's Society in the world. It surely is the oldest in North America. The local group's purpose was to provide charity to anyone who needed it, regardless of nationality. At first only open to people of Scottish lineage, it soon opened to non-Scots. After the Revolutionary War, loyalists and patriots reportedly reunited harmoniously as they elected patriot Gen. William Moultrie as president and two loyalists as officers. The society's hall, built in 1815, was where South Carolina's Ordinance of Secession was adopted in 1860. The hall burned the following year. It has since shared a home with the S.C. Society at its hall on Meeting Street. – *AB*

ENGLAND EUROPE AFRICA

ATLANTIC OCEAN

45

Charleston earned its nickname due to its religious tolerance

Throughout its early years, Charles Town was attacked from sea and land by France, Spain, pirates and Native Americans. Settlers arrived from England and were later followed by immigrants from Scotland, France, Germany, Ireland and more, bringing multiple Protestant denominations, Judaism and Roman Catholicism. It was this conglomeration of religious backgrounds and religious tolerance that earned colonial Charleston its moniker of the Holy City. Charleston's tolerance, however, only went so far. From the beginning of the Carolina colony, Europeans also imported enslaved Africans, who wove additional layers into what became the culture of the Lowcountry. – *SB*

46

Archaeological digs reveal the lives of early Charlestonians

Nearly every historical structure in Charleston contains an archaeological component below the ground. Layers of soil and sediment cover artifacts and relics of the colonial city like chamber pots, pipe stems, cups and saucers. Exploration of residential sites has revealed the crowded noisy features that characterize colonial cities, such as kitchens, slaves' quarters, carriage houses, stables, wells, drains and more. – *SB*

47

Piracy was a problem for some early Charlestonians

Edward Teach, otherwise known as the pirate Blackbeard, appeared off the coast of Charles Town with a flotilla of four ships in 1718. At the time, it was the most powerful naval force in the hemisphere. Teach seized several Carolina ships and captured councilman Samuel Wragg, his son and other residents, demanding ransoms of money and medicine. Blackbeard blockaded Charles Town harbor for a week and eventually all ransoms were paid. The pirate then sailed north, plundering along the way until he reached Virginia, where his reputation for invincibility came to an end when authorities captured and executed him. – *SB*

48

Pirates hanged in White Point Garden

A stone marker at White Point Garden near Charleston's Battery memorializes the hanging of 49 pirates in 1718. While local historian Nic Butler says there is a "frustrating paucity of details" in historical documents, the exact location of the public hanging is hard to pinpoint because the topography of the site has changed much in the last three centuries. The marker provides this detail:

"Near this spot in the autumn of 1718, Stede Bonnet, notorious 'gentleman pirate,' and twenty nine of his men, captured by Colonel William Rhett, met their just deserts (sic) after a trial and charge, famous in American history, by Chief Justice Nicholas Trott. Later, nineteen of Richard Worley's crew, captured by Governor Robert Johnson, were also found guilty and hanged. All were buried off White Point Garden, in the marsh beyond low-water mark." – *AB*

Early fires caused big losses, anxiety

Throughout more than three centuries, fire has shaped Charleston's history. Early settlers lost about 50 buildings – one third of those in the new settlement – in 1698. "The city quickly developed building standards that included brick chimneys and levied a tax on residents that would be used for ladders and buckets. A few years later, Charles Town elected a board of fire masters to supervise firefighting efforts and to enforce the new building codes. But soon, night watchmen grew neglectful; laws and building codes were left unenforced; and fires continued to rage," according to the *Hartsville News Journal.* The Great Fire of 1740, fueled by turpentine, tar and rum, destroyed warehouses on the waterfront. And it caused the failure of the nation's first fire insurance company, The Friendly Society in Charleston. – *AB*

50

Charleston and its surrounding area bear the names of some important folks

The original Lords Proprietors of Carolina, powerful men granted royal charters for the establishment of governance of an English colony in the 17th century, have names that are familiar to Charleston-area residents. A few of these names include John Berkeley, for which Berkeley County is named; Anthony Ashley Cooper, for whom two rivers are named; and George Monck, for whom Moncks Corner is named. – *SB*

51

Rice: Agricultural gold for S.C. planters

Rice, the crop that made many early South Carolina planters rich, was first grown in the colony on Charleston's peninsula in the 1690s. "By the 1720s thousands of West Africans familiar with the crop had been brought to the colony to provide both the skills and hard labor necessary to build dikes and convert tens of thousands of acres of tidal marshes into rice fields," according to a history by Jack Bass and Scott Poole. Rice dominated the state's economy for almost 200 years. The nation's leading rice producer before the Revolution, around 1700, the colony produced an average of 130 tons of rice annually, which grew to an annual average of more than 66 million pounds between 1768 and 1772. But domination didn't last thanks to competitors in other states, the devastation of the Civil War and hurricanes in the early 20th century. By 1919, annual production was about 4 million pounds, just 3 percent of what it was before the Civil War. – *AB*

52

Eliza Lucas Pinckney, indigo pioneer and mother of a patriot

When Eliza Lucas Pinckney (1722-1793) was in her early 20s, she demonstrated that Carolina planters could successfully grow indigo as a profitable cash crop. "Her efforts were instrumental in alerting other planters to greater profitability, and she gave away indigo seeds 'in small quantities to a great number of people' in the area," according to *The South Carolina Encyclopedia.* In 1744, the year indigo turned the corner as a crop, Lucas married Charles Pinckney, an attorney and member of the Royal Council. Though 20 years her senior, Pinckney and Eliza had four children, including Charles Cotesworth Pinckney, a soldier, diplomat and one of three South Carolina signers of the U.S. Constitution, and Thomas Pinckney, who became a governor, diplomat and congressman. Eliza Pinckney died in Philadelphia of cancer. – *AB*

53

Indigo was an early colonial cash crop

Indigo, a plant used to make blue dye, was a big deal in colonial South Carolina. It was a money crop that helped to drive the 18th century economy. First grown successfully by plantation owner Eliza Lucas Pinckney in what is now the West Ashley part of Charleston, indigo became second only to rice in export value, according to *The South Carolina Encyclopedia.* While South Carolina planters experimented with indigo production in the early days of the colony, it was reintroduced in the 1740s when war cut off the British supply from the French West Indies. – *AB*

54

Indigo was second only to rice in importance in the colony

Indigo was second only to rice in export value in the Charleston of the 18th century. By 1747, in its early days of cultivation, colonists exported 138,000 pounds of dye. By 1775, production peaked at 1.12 million pounds. The fifth most valuable commodity exported by Britain's mainland colonies, indigo production was successful because, in part, it fit well within the existing agricultural economy and could be grown on land not suited for rice. Planters and farmers already committed to plantation agriculture did not have to reconfigure their land and labor. Though the Continental Army used Carolina indigo to dye some of its uniforms, the Revolutionary War disrupted the crop's production, with exports declining sharply in the 1790s. By 1802, it was no longer listed among Carolina's exports. – *SB*

55

Early naturalists important for Charleston, region

Not to be missed as important naturalist contributors in the early days of the colony were Mark Catesby, Elizabeth Lamboll, Alexander Garden and Andre Michaux. Catesby, an English illustrator and naturalist, arrived in the Holy City in 1722 and spent several years researching and documenting native plants in a book still appreciated today. Lamboll, who lived on King Street, had a garden that included many varieties of orange trees and hosted early American botanist and explorer John Bartram in 1765. Aptly-named Garden, a doctor born in Scotland in 1730 who moved to Charleston in 1752, wrote extensively about natural history and had the gardenia (*Gardenia jasminoides*) that blooms fragrantly in Lowcountry gardens each May named for him. Botanist Michaux, who bought 120 acres of land in 1786 that is now the location of the Charleston International Airport, introduced several plants to the area, including the mimosa, crape myrtle, tea olive, Chinese tallow and the Ginkgo tree. – *AB*

56

Great Fire of 1740

A huge fire ripped through about half of the city of Charleston in 1740, burning 300 homes and buildings in several blocks along the waterfront south of Broad Street and along Elliott, Union (now State) and Church streets. In the early days of the colony, fire was such a worry and danger that several businessmen in 1736 organized the first fire insurance company, the Friendly Society for the Mutual Insuring of Homes against Fire at Charles Town. "The insurance company prospered with a fund of approximately 100,000 pounds sterling until 1740, when a disastrous fire forced the Friendly Society into bankruptcy," according to a book by Keith Krawczynski. – *AB*

57

Charleston Library Society is nation's third oldest library

The Charleston Library Society, the nation's third oldest library, got started in 1748 when 19 men in various trades wanted the latest publications from Great Britain. Its collection, now a repository of rare books, manuscripts, documents, maps and more, is available to members and researchers. The library's holdings seeded the founding of the College of Charleston in 1770 and the core collection of artifacts for the first museum in America, the Charleston Museum, in 1773. Located on King Street since 1914, it continues to fulfill its mission of providing educational opportunities; preserving, sharing and expanding its collection; improving access to collections through technology; offering lectures and programs of interest; collaborating with other cultural organizations; and maintaining an archival center that serves scholars, researchers and students. The society is a membership organization. – *AB*

58

Ansonborough is first suburb

Ansonborough became Charleston's first suburb in the 1740s after a sea captain named George Anson reportedly bought a 64-acre tract of land in 1726 from his winnings at cards. In the early days, Boundary Street (now Calhoun Street) served as the northern border with an area between Society and Wentworth streets as the area's southern boundary. The tract's western boundary was King Street while its eastern line was the Cooper River. Many of the houses today date to the 1840s after a devastating fire in 1838. After World War II, the Historic Charleston Foundation began a rehabilitation project to restore many houses that had fallen into slum-like condition. – *AB*

59

German Friendly Society founded by St. John's Lutheran congregation

Known as the "Mother Church of Lutheranism" in South Carolina, St. John's Lutheran Church, on the corner of Archdale and Clifford Streets, has a long history of community involvement and support. Members of the congregation founded the German Friendly Society in 1766 to help new American immigrants and give aid to widows and orphans. Originally comprised of 16 German men, they constituted themselves as a social and mutual-assistance society to pay sick and death benefits. Almost immediately after its founding, the German ethnicity requirement for membership was lifted, as was the need to speak German. – *SB*

60

Thomas Elfe, master cabinetmaker

One of the most acclaimed cabinetmakers of his day, Thomas Elfe (1719-1775) was a prolific craftsman during his career. A contemporary of Great Britain's Thomas Chippendale, Elfe was considered Charleston's best furniture maker of the 18th century, with one historian saying he made some of the finest furniture produced in the period. After an apprenticeship in England and inheritance of his uncle's money and tools, Elfe moved to the colonies, setting up shop in 1746 in Charleston. By the end of his career, he and employees annually made about 200 pieces of furniture, including detailed cabinets, stacking chests, double chests of drawers and more in Georgian, Rococo, Gothic and other styles. Many were sold to wealthy planters and merchants. Today, his pieces are found in the Governor's Mansion in Columbia, the Charleston Museum and other museums. Elfe's house (1760) at 54 Queen St. was restored in the 1990s. – *AB*

61

How the pineapple came to be a symbol of hospitality

The story of the pineapple as an icon of hospitality can be traced back to early colonial Charlestowne, when it was a prominent port city. The fruit represented the exotic lands that captains sailed to and it became a symbol itself of faraway places. Sailors arriving home from long voyages at sea would spear a pineapple to symbolize they had returned safely. It was also an open invitation for neighbors to come and enjoy a meal or a drink and exchange stories. Today, relief sculptures of pineapples can still be found in stonework and iron-wrought gates throughout the city as symbols of hospitality. – *SB*

CP

The wars: Revolutionary and Civil

62

South Carolina's flag looks just a bit different

South Carolina's highly-recognizable state flag, based on one of the first Revolutionary War flags, invariably includes a white palmetto and crescent design on a blue background. State law, however, does not provide any specifications for "the shape, size, design or placement" of the symbols or of the exact color of the background. Therefore, flags from different manufacturers may appear differently. A state Senate committee met in January 2018 to standardize the design, but no formal measures were taken. The legislature, however, formed a study committee to explore designs to be considered for official use. The committee reported its findings in March 2020, revisiting a 1910 sketch by Charleston native and amateur artist Ellen Heyward Jervey and drawing inspiration from it for the official design pitch. – *SB*

63

How the palmetto tree was added to the state flag

South Carolina's Revolutionary Council of Safety asked Colonel William Moultrie to design a flag in 1775 for the state troops in preparation for the American Revolutionary War. The flag's original design had the blue of the militia's uniforms and a crescent, which some scholars say was really a military gorget. The palmetto was added in 1861 as a reference to Moultrie's defense of Sullivan's Island, the fortress on which had survived largely due to the ability of interwoven fibers of palmetto trees to absorb cannon fire and, thus, to withstand British attacks. – *SB*

The first British attempt to capture Charleston was fought over Sullivan's Island

The British organized an expedition in early 1776 for operations in the rebellious southern colonies of North America, but were delayed by logistics and bad weather. When they arrived at the coast of North Carolina in May, British General Henry Clinton and Admiral Sir Peter Parker decided instead to act against Charleston. They reached the harbor in early June and troops landed on Long Island, now called the Isle of Palms, before preparing for a naval bombardment and land assault on Fort Sullivan, an adjacent island. Both proved ineffective, as Breach Inlet, the channel between the two islands, was too deep to wade, and American defenses prevented an amphibious landing. Moreover, the sand and palmetto log construction of the fort prevented significant damage from the British bombardment. – *SB*

Carolina Day commemorates the historic battle over Sullivan's Island

After the tumultuous and wildly significant battle on June 28, 1776, at Fort Sullivan, the battle for American independence was pushed northward, and Charleston settled into a period of relative peace and prosperity. However, the people of Charleston vowed the importance of the battle was not to be forgotten. In May the following year, a group of men formed the Palmetto Society to commemorate the "signal and providential victory obtained by our gallant troops over the formidable fleet and army of Great Britain at Sullivan's Island." Some community members had apparently referred to the annual celebration as "Palmetto Day," but in 1873, nearly a century later, the newspapers of Charleston proudly announced a more robust observance for the holiday, dubbing it "Carolina Day," and it continues to be celebrated each year. – *SB*

66

College of Charleston founders help start a nation

What does the College of Charleston and the United States have in common? Six men: three future signers of the Declaration of Independence and three future signers of the United States Constitution helped found Charleston College in 1770. The College of Charleston founders who also signed the Declaration of Independence include Edward Rutledge, Arthur Middleton and Thomas Heyward. The founders that also signed the Constitution include John Rutledge, Charles Pinckney and Charles Cotesworth Pinckney. Other founders of the college were or became federal and state lawmakers and judges, state governors, diplomats, and Charleston councilmen and mayors. – *LS*

67

The second British attempt to take Charleston

The British made a second attempt to capture Charleston in 1779 while the main American Army was in Georgia. British Gen. Augustine Prevost marched from Savannah to Charleston, but as Gen. William Moultrie's small force was holding its own, the Continental Army returned from Georgia, fighting back the British. – *SB*

Third attempt was biggest colonial loss of Revolutionary War

The Redcoats mounted their strongest attempt to take the Holy City in 1780 when Sir Henry Clinton's 10,000-man army, supported by the Royal Navy, laid siege to the city from April 1 to May 12. It was the longest siege of the Revolutionary War. It ended when Charleston and 6,000 colonial soldiers surrendered. The loss is considered the worst defeat of the Continental Army during the Revolutionary War and gave the British a foothold to try to retake the Southern states, a quest that ultimately failed. – *SB and AB*

Thousands of slaves fled to the British in 1782

Throughout the Revolutionary War, slaves fled to the British, seeking freedom. Many served as laborers or soldiers. As the British evacuated the Charleston port in 1782, there's evidence that as many as 10,000 slaves were taken from the area despite protests by state officials and owners. While the British reportedly promised freedom to slaves for their loyalty, their fate varied, according to historian Bernard E. Powers Jr. Those who made it to Canada, Sierra Leone and London often obtained promised freedom. But "some were taken to the Caribbean where they were resold, perhaps into an even harsher form of slavery." – *AB*

70

Charleston's three Fort Moultries

Sullivan Island's protective sand and palmetto log structure was under construction during a nine-hour British attack on June 28, 1776. The fort stood its ground against Commodore Sir Peter Parker and nine British men-of-war ships. It was the first major victory of the Revolutionary War and reportedly inspired founding fathers to sign the Declaration of Independence. The fort later was named to honor the patriots' commander, Col. William Moultrie. But the fort fell into ruin from neglect after the war. A second Fort Moultrie was constructed a few years later, during a war between the British and the French in 1793. The second fort again fell victim to neglect, and was finally destroyed by a hurricane in 1804. By 1807, with many of the new United States military installations in need of repair, the federal government authorized funding of a third Fort Moultrie, the construction of which finished in 1809 on Sullivan's Island. – *SB*

71

Leading patriot: Christopher Gadsden

Christopher Gadsden (1724-1805) was a well-to-do Charleston merchant and planter who defied British authority years before the Revolutionary War. A stalwart advocate for American home rule, he joined the Sons of Liberty and helped to lead Charleston's patriot party. Elected to the First Continental Congress, he returned to South Carolina in 1776 to serve as a colonel of the state's First Regiment as well as in the Provincial Congress, where he co-authored the state's constitution. He reportedly had an "irrational temperament" as lieutenant governor which may have led to the loss of more than 2,000 Continental troops when Charleston fell to the British in 1780. After 10 months in prison, he came home to Charleston to rebuild his businesses, returning to public service only briefly to vote to ratify the U.S. Constitution. He is buried in St. Philip's Churchyard. – *AB*

72

Gadsden's flag: Don't tread on me

A yellow flag with a coiled rattlesnake above the words "Don't Tread on Me" is a Revolutionary War symbol for national unity and perseverance that is attributed to Charleston patriot Christopher Gadsden. In 1754, founding father Ben Franklin penned what's thought to be the colonies' first political cartoon with a rattlesnake cut into eight pieces over the words, "Join, or Die," to rally colonists to fight with the British in the French and Indian War. Fast forward 21 years when Gadsden, a member of the Second Continental Congress, was on a committee to outfit the colonies' first naval mission. He presented the yellow flag to the new Navy's commander to be his personal standard, or flag, for the ship. Gadsden's flag later inspired the first U.S. Navy Jack, a red-and-white striped flag with the rattlesnake. In the 21st century, the yellow flag was used by tea party enthusiasts to show their anger at government – not support as it was intended more than 200 years ago. – *AB*

73

Plaque marks the original site of the Liberty Tree in downtown Charleston

Christopher Gadsden first advocated for colonial independence from the British in 1766 under a live oak that would come to be known as the Liberty Tree. A bronze plaque by the Sons of the Revolution marks the spot where the tree once stood. Gadsden, along with his fellow revolutionaries, led public meetings to protest the British Stamp Act and tea tax, calling themselves the Sons of Liberty. However, the British later cut the tree down and burned the stump. – *SB*

74

Guess who got a cane head from the Liberty Tree?

So here's where the story about the Liberty Tree gets interesting. When the British occupied Charleston from 1780 to 1782, they cut down the Liberty Tree and burned its stump to prevent it from becoming a patriot shrine. But they didn't think about the tree's pesky roots. After the war, Judge William Johnson retrieved a root and had it made into cane heads. One of them was given to Thomas Jefferson, author of the Declaration of Independence. Pretty neat, huh? – *AB*

75

Leading patriot: Henry Laurens

Henry Laurens, born in Charleston in 1724, served as a president of the Continental Congress. A planter made wealthy through trading Carolina rice and indigo—and slaves—he later served, in many ways, as the Revolution's banker, becoming the only American to ever be imprisoned in the Tower of London. His oldest son, John, served as an important aide-de-camp to General George Washington in the Revolutionary War. Henry Laurens died in 1792. – *AB*

76

Leading patriot: Charles Pinckney

Charles Pinckney (1757-1824), one of four South Carolinians who helped draft the U.S. Constitution, was instrumental in promoting the state's history of religious tolerance by urging no religious tests for anyone holding office in the fledgling nation. Born into a planter family, Pinckney was the youngest and a controversial delegate to the constitutional convention, submitting a constitutional framework in 1787 called the "Pinckney Draft," which argued for a strong, central government. Long involved in state and national politics, Pinckney later served three terms as governor as well as being a U.S. senator and member of the U.S. House of Representatives.– *AB*

77

Leading patriot: Charles Cotesworth Pinckney

Not to be confused with cousin Charles Pinckney, Charles Cotesworth Pinckney (1746-1825) was a signer of the U.S. Constitution who was born in Charleston into an aristocratic family. His father, Charles, was a lawyer on South Carolina's provincial council, and his mother was Eliza Lucas Pinckney, who introduced indigo as a cash crop. In the Revolutionary era, Pinckney commanded a regiment in the Battle of Sullivan's Island and later served as an aide de camp for General George Washington. As a constitutional framer, Pinckney, "ardently and ably defended the exporting and slaveholding interests of southern planters," according to the *S.C. Encyclopedia.* He served as a minister to France during Washington's presidency and later was twice a presidential candidate for the Federalist Party. – *AB*

78

Signer's house still standing

A 1763 house built by John Rutledge, a signer of the U.S. Constitution, governor of South Carolina and briefly, chief justice of the U.S. Supreme Court, is a national historic landmark. Completed in 1763, the house incorporates two carriage houses in addition to the distinctive home. Now converted into a hotel, the John Rutledge House Inn is one of only 15 homes of signers of the Constitution that still stand today. In 2020, readers of *Travel + Leisure* magazine voted it the second best hotel in Charleston and 12th best city hotel in the nation. – *SB*

79

In fact, it's the only founding father's house you can sleep in!

The house that patriot John Rutledge built on Broad Street near King Street for his wife, Elizabeth Grimke, today is an inn, thanks to a 1989 restoration. The home, which was visited by George Washington during his 1791 presidential trip to Charleston, survived a great fire during the Civil War, and took a hit from a Union cannon. It's the only house in the country of a drafter of the U.S. Constitution where you can stay overnight as a guest! – *CH*

U.S. Constitution signed in S.C. at Old Exchange and Provost Dungeon

One Charleston landmark, the Old Exchange and Provost Dungeon, was completed in 1771 and has seen some of the most significant moments in the state's history, including being one of only four surviving structures that served as the site of the ratification of the U.S. Constitution. Over the last 250 years, it has been a commercial exchange, post office, city hall, military headquarters and museum. Today, the Old Exchange is owned by the South Carolina State Society of the Daughters of the American Revolution and operated by the City of Charleston. – *SB*

81

Charleston leaders help to frame nation's future

Because Charleston was such a wealthy port in the days leading to the Revolutionary War, her leaders were key to the cause of liberty. Charleston's four signers of the Declaration of Independence (1776) were Thomas Heyward Jr.; Thomas Lynch Jr., the second youngest signer at age 26; Edward Rutledge, the youngest signer; and Arthur Middleton. Heyward, Rutledge and Middleton were captured by the British in 1780 and sent to prison in St. Augustine, Fla. Charleston's four signers of the U.S. Constitution were Pierce Butler; Charles Pinckney; his cousin, Charles Cotesworth Pinckney and John Rutledge, older brother of Edward. – *AB*

82

Some streets have patriotic names

A section of old Charleston called the Village of Washington has street names that honor local patriots and the American cause: Congress, Gadsden, Huger, Moultrie, Pinckney and President. City fathers laid out the street from King Street westward. Its southern boundary was Line Street and its northern edge was at the Washington Race Course, which is Hampton Park today.– *AB*

83

War of 1812 has little impact on Charleston or South Carolina

While Charleston was a cauldron of patriotic fervor and leadership in the Revolutionary War, the War of 1812 bypassed the Palmetto State as there were no battles or skirmishes in the state. While Charlestonians feared an invasion like the one in 1780, none occurred. South Carolinians did, however, participate by assembling more than 5,000 soldiers for the national effort, upgrading coastal defenses and raising more than a half million dollars for defense. – *AB*

85

Immigrant's rice mill design spread across the Lowcountry

Jonathan Lucas, born in 1754 in Cumberland, England, immigrated to South Carolina, where he was put to work by a Santee River rice planter to improve the output of his plantation's rice mill. Within a short time, Lucas's experiments with wind and water as power sources came to fruition, with a new pounding mill design powered by an undershot waterwheel fed by a mill pond. He continued to improve his design, building his first tide-powered mill in 1791. It was highly automated and only needed three workers to operate. Alongside his son, Jonathan Jr., Lucas built his rice mills throughout the Lowcountry and purchased his own plantation on Shem Creek, where he established his own rice and sawmilling operation. In 1817, Lucas built the first steam-powered rice mill in the United States. – *SB*

Lucas Jr. also had a successful career as a millwright

Jonathan Lucas's son, Jonathan Jr., went on to make a name for himself as a millwright after working with his father to build rice mills throughout the Lowcountry. He patented an improved rice-cleaning machine in 1808 that became a highly-successful industrial innovation across English and western Europe. About this time, he also built a three-story Adamesque-style house and outbuildings on Calhoun Street which today are part of medical complexes in the area. Lucas Jr.'s son, Jonathan Lucas III, built the state's largest antebellum rice mill, West Point Mills, in 1839 along the Ashley River. – *SB*

86

Calhoun has three important links to Charleston

South Carolina's fiery John C. Calhoun served in public office for almost 40 years – in Congress (1811-17), as U.S. Secretary of War (1817-25), as vice president (1825-1832), as a United States senator (1832-43 and 1845-50) and as U.S. Secretary of State (1844-45). Born in Abbeville, he had three links to Charleston. First, he read law in the Holy City with attorney William Henry DeSaussure, a prominent Federalist, before returning to home to practice law and go into politics. Second, known as a war hawk, Calhoun later developed the political idea of nullification as a way for states to suspend federal laws they deemed unconstitutional and he used the legal construct to advocate for slavery, which helped to tear the country apart before he died in 1850. His third tie to Charleston: A statue of him loomed for more than a century over Marion Square. It was removed in 2020 after a vote by Charleston City Council. Calhoun is buried in St. Philip's Churchyard in Charleston. – *AB*

87

Audubon lived in Charleston while working on a masterpiece

John James Audubon (1785-1851), born as Jean-Jacques Rabine Fougere in Haiti, was a naturalist, ornithologist and painter whose major work, *The Birds of America* (1827-38), is a a four-volume folio with 435 hand-colored engravings. It is considered one of the finest ornithological works ever completed. Charleston played an important part in the creation of the color-plate book because of Audubon's friendship with Lutheran minister and fellow naturalist John Bachman. "Audubon made Bachman's home the center of his work in America," according to the *South Carolina Encyclopedia.* "There he had a studio and space to prepare and draw specimens, and he was assisted by Maria Martin, Bachman's sister-in-law, who painted botanical settings for his paintings. Audubon also sold subscriptions to *The Birds of America* to the Charleston Library Society and South Carolina College." – *AB*

South Carolina is the first state to secede

Just after 9 p.m. on Dec. 20, 1860, South Carolina became the first state to secede from the United States in South Carolina Institute Hall after a "Convention of the People," called by the General Assembly, in St. Andrew's Hall on Broad Street. The original convention was meant to be held in Columbia, but fears of a smallpox outbreak led the 169 delegates to move the meeting to Charleston. Posters entitled "The Union is Dissolved" flooded the streets and joyful crowds celebrated after the decision. – *SB*

No deaths during "shots heard around the world"

On April 12, 1861, Confederates opened fire on Fort Sumter at 4:30 a.m. from multiple positions surrounding the fort – but not from the peninsula as many believe. Thousands of spectators filled rooftops and lined the Battery to watch the barrage. After the 34-hour bombardment, Union Major Robert Anderson, commander of Fort Sumter, surrendered. Incredibly, no one died during the engagement in which more than 3,000 shells were fired. It wasn't until an accidental explosion during the surrender ceremony that the first casualty of the Civil War, Daniel Hough, a Union soldier, was claimed. – *SB*

90

Fort Sumter remained an important bastion after the first barrage

Confederate forces continued to occupy Fort Sumter, using it to hold a defense of Charleston Harbor after P.G.T. Beauregard captured the bastion in 1861. Better armed and finally finished, the fort allowed the Southern military to create a valuable hole in the Union blockade of the Atlantic seaboard. Two years later, in 1863, the Union would launch its first assault against Fort Sumter, when Rear Admiral Samuel Francis Du Pont attempted a naval attack on the port city of Charleston. He arrived in Charleston with a fleet of nine ironclad warships, but in collaboration with Fort Sumter, Confederate batteries commanded by Beauregard unleashed a barrage of cannon fire against the fleet, dealing over 500 hits and forcing the fleet to retreat. – *SB*

91

The Battery protects the city

When the Civil War broke out, the Battery was a sea wall at the southern tip of the Charleston peninsula that was used as a fortification for the Holy City. More than 100 years earlier in 1737, Broughton's Battery (also known as Fort Wilkins) was erected on Oyster Point and later an earthwork sea wall was built along the Cooper and Ashley rivers. While the fort was demolished in 1789, the sea walls were progressively strengthened, and by the time the stone and masonry sea wall was completed in 1820, the wall was commonly known as The Battery. – *CH*

92

Why you don't see a lot of modern architecture in Charleston

During the American Civil War, there was one name that struck fear in the hearts of Southerners across the Confederacy – William Tecumseh Sherman. The Union general led his troops out of what remained of Atlanta on Nov. 16, 1864, and rumor had it that he was headed toward Charleston on what became known as the March to the Sea. In truth, the only thing anyone knew for sure was that he was marching toward the ocean, but locals in the Lowcountry assumed that the Holy City was his target because the first shots of the Civil War were fired here. As it happened, Sherman made it to Savannah, which he "gave" to President Abraham Lincoln as a Christmas present in 1864. His forces then headed north to Columbia, leaving Charleston to fate.– *SB*

CP

The civil rights era

93

The journey from slaving wharf to International African American Museum

The Gadsden's Wharf slaving complex, located near the S.C. Aquarium on the Cooper River in Charleston, was completed in the 1770s. The complex, which could hold up to 1,000 enslaved Africans, featured an 840-foot river wharf that could dock six ships. From 1783 until 1807, an estimated 100,000 enslaved West Africans passed into the United States through the wharf. Today more than 200 years later, it is the site of the International African American Museum, which took decades of planning to bring to fruition. The museum broke ground in fall 2019 – the 400th anniversary of the start of slavery in America. Fueled by tens of millions of dollars of donations, it will tell the stories of enslaved people who were forced from their homelands to be treated as inhumane for centuries. It also seeks to tell the stories of triumph. It is expected to open in 2022. – *LS*

94

Denmark Vesey becomes abolitionist hero

A founder of Emanuel AME Church, Denmark Vesey was born into slavery but purchased his freedom in 1799. In 1822, he was accused of planning a large rebellion of former slaves and free blacks to coincide with Bastille Day in Charleston. The plan called for the execution of slave masters and, in the aftermath, slaves would sail to Haiti. But two slaves leaked details of the plot before it could get underway and Vesey was rounded up with 130 other men. Sixty-seven were convicted and 37 were hanged, including Vesey, who died July 2, 1822. Vesey became a symbol for abolitionists, including Frederick Douglass, during the Civil War. Some 20th and 21st century historians have questioned whether the plot was actually a plot or if it was just "angry talk," however. A statue honoring Vesey is in Hampton Park in Charleston today. – *LS*

95

Payne opens school in 1829 for Black children in Charleston

Daniel Alexander Payne, born in 1811 in Charleston to free Black parents, opened a school for Black children in 1829. He was 19. Six years later, the state legislature passed a bill that forced him to close the school. He went on to become a bishop in the African Methodist Episcopal church. In 1882 – 73 years before Rosa Parks gained fame for refusing to move on an Alabama bus – a train conductor told Payne, a passenger headed to a Florida church conference, that he had to ride on a railroad car reserved for "colored passengers." Payne replied: "I will not dishonor my manhood by going into that car." The train was stopped and Payne was ultimately removed. He died in 1893. – *LS*

Robert Smalls's escape from slavery happens in Charleston waters

Robert Smalls, a key South Carolina figure of the Civil War and years of Reconstruction that followed, was born into slavery in 1839 in Beaufort. In 1862, he and his Black crew were left aboard the Confederate ship *Planter* in the Charleston harbor. They commandeered the ship and sailed it to the U.S. blockade surrounding the Confederate-controlled waters. The ship then became a Union warship. After the war, in 1868, Smalls worked as a Republican delegate with the state legislature to establish the state's first free and compulsory public school system in the United States. In 1875, Smalls was elected to the U.S. Congress. He died in 1915. – *LS*

97

Charleston's Ransier was state's first Black lieutenant governor

Alonzo J. Ransier was born a free person of color in Charleston in 1834. Immediately following the Civil War, he was elected to the state legislature. In 1870, Ransier became the state's first Black lieutenant governor, defeating ex-Confederate Gen. M.C. Butler at the polls. As lieutenant governor, he became known for his honesty amidst a corrupt executive branch. In 1873, he became a congressman for the state for a single term. In the late 1870s, Ransier lapsed into poverty and obscurity as he worked as a night watchman in a customs house and as a municipal street sweeper in Charleston. He lapsed into poverty in 1880 and died in obscurity two years later. – *LS*

98

Avery Normal Institute continues its lasting legacy

The Avery Normal Institute, founded in 1865 as a private school and established by the New York-based American Missionary Association (AMA), was the first accredited secondary school for African Americans in Charleston. The school's second principal, Francis Cardozo, campaigned to have a permanent building constructed, where the school added teacher training to its mission. Graduates taught in one-room schoolhouses all over the state, especially in the Lowcountry, despite being prohibited from teaching in all but one of Charleston's Black public schools. After the school's closure in 1954, the Avery Institute of Afro-American History and Culture was established in 1978 to save the original school building, and joined the College of Charleston to found the Avery Research Center for African American History and Culture. Today, the Avery Institute continues as a hub of African American scholarship. – *SB*

99

Cannon Street Hospital trained Black doctors, nurses

The Hospital and Training School for Nurses of Charleston, also known as the Cannon Street Hospital, was established in 1897 as a training ground for Black doctors and nurses. But it also provided care to white and Black patients equally. The Hospital and Training School for Nurses was the first hospital in South Carolina established for nurse training for Black people and the ninth Black institution of its kind in the country, according to the Waring Historical Library at the Medical University of South Carolina. When the hospital relocated to Courtenay Street, it was renamed in honor of Dr. Alonzo C. McClennan and Anna DeCosta Banks as the McClennan-Banks Memorial Hospital. – *LS*

100

Local artist founds local NAACP, enacts change in state law

Edwin Harleston, a noted artist born in 1882 in Charleston, won a scholarship to the Avery Normal Institute and graduated as valedictorian in 1900. He went on to continue his schooling at Atlanta University, Harvard University, the School of Fine Arts in Boston, and, finally, at the Renouard Training School for Embalmers, which he finished in 1917. Soon after, he became a founding member of the Charleston chapter of the National Association for the Advancement of Colored People (NAACP) and served as its first president. Two years later, he organized a campaign and petition drive that would ultimately result in the change of state law, allowing Black teachers to teach in Charleston's Black public schools. – *SB*.

101

Lynchers convicted after 1919 race riots

The Charleston race riots of 1919 resulted in one of the few known cases where white lynchers in the South were convicted. From April through October in Charleston and a dozen cities across the U.S., anxious white residents balked at a newfound assertiveness demonstrated by the Black servicemen returning from World War I. In May, rumors spread in Charleston that a Black man shot a white sailor. Several white servicemen attacked a Black passerby, prompting other blacks to respond with gunfire. In the confrontation, three Black men died and 24 – white and Black – were wounded. The city went under martial law, and Mayor Tristian Hyde made several concessions to the newly-formed Charleston branch of the NAACP. A Naval investigation found that four U.S. sailors and one civilian – all white men – initiated the riot. Most charges, from murder and rioting and to assaulting police officers, were dropped for both white and Black men. In the end, only eight men received $50 fines for carrying a concealed weapon. – *LS*

102

Son of a Confederate soldier becomes early figure in civil rights

As a federal judge in 1940s and 1950s Charleston, Julius Waties Waring paved the way for several key civil rights victories. Born in 1880 as the son of a Confederate soldier, Waring became an establishment lawyer in Charleston. But after being appointed to the federal bench late in his career, he soon found himself championing equal rights for African Americans. His judgment on the 1951 *Briggs v. Elliott* case was the first time a federal judge challenged the "separate but equal" education rule since *Plessy v. Ferguson* in 1896. He also presided over a 1944 case in which a Black teacher sought pay equal to white teachers, and a 1947 case that challenged the S.C. Democratic Party's prohibition on Black participation. In both cases, he sided with plaintiffs. The voting access case led to threats on the judge's life. Waring, ostracized by Charleston society, left the city for New York when he retired in 1954. He died Jan. 11, 1968. – *LS*

103

Cigar Factory Strike sparked by discrimination in 1945

On East Bay Street on the peninsula, the Cigar Factory retail complex that operates today as offices and shops is the namesake of its original purpose: a cigar factory. In October 1945, it became the site of an early civil rights protest when 1,000 employees walked off their jobs in response to persistent racial discrimination, inadequate pay and poor health benefits. Most of the striking workers were Black women. They demanded a pay increase of 25 cents per hour and the ability to unionize. The strike lasted five months. To maintain morale, the workers sang the notable civil rights hymn, "We Shall Overcome." In an agreement that ended the strike, workers received an 8-cent hourly raise and received back pay. They also saw the removal of restrictions barring African Americans from skilled jobs. – *LS*

104

Septima Clark promotes citizenship schools across South

The name "Septima Poinsette Clark" continues to inspire reverence in Charleston's activist community. Born in 1898 in the Holy City, she was so respected for her work in the civil rights movement for spreading voter education through citizenship schools that Dr. Martin Luther King Jr. asked her to accompany him to Norway in 1964 when he accepted the Nobel Peace Prize. Clark was a school teacher from 1916 when she was 18 until she and 41 others were fired 40 years later for being members of the NAACP. As the civil rights movement blossomed, she became director of workshops at the Highlander School in Monteagle, Tenn., an integrated training center where people learned about civil rights. One of her students was Rosa Parks. Then she spread citizenship schools through work with King and the Southern Christian Leadership Council. By 1970, an estimated 1.7 million blacks registered to vote in the South. She died in 1987 in Charleston. – *AB*

105

Esau Jenkins: "Love is progress, Hate is expensive"

Esau Jenkins, a seminal Lowcountry civil rights pioneer, owned a green Volkswagen microbus that ferried African Americans on Charleston's sea islands to work, school and the voting polls. Today, that van, emblazoned with the hand-painted words "Love is progress, Hate is expensive," is on permanent exhibit in the Smithsonian National Museum of African American History and Culture, which opened in 2016. Born on Johns Island in 1910, Jenkins started The Progressive Club in 1948 as a small, cooperative store that matured into a center for political, social, educational and recreational activities for the area's Black residents. Its citizenship school pioneered large-scale voter registration across the Jim Crow South. Jenkins, who rubbed shoulders with luminaries like Dr. Martin Luther King Jr., died in 1972. – *AB*

106

The beginning of the end of segregated schools

An important South Carolina case, *Briggs v. Elliott*, filed in Clarendon County in 1951 came to shape the landmark 1954 *Brown v. Board of Education* decision by the U.S. Supreme Court that eventually ended the policy of public school segregation. The South Carolina case, filed because Black parents in the Summerton area wanted the local school district to pay for gas to bus their children to school, was heard in federal court in Charleston by U.S. District Judge J. Waties Waring and two other judges. In an appellate dissent that shocked the state, Waring wrote that separate education – segregation – was not equal, as had been allowed for generations. The *Briggs* case then was bundled with *Brown* and three other cases and went to the U.S. Supreme Court as it engaged to settle public school segregation. Waring's dissent in the *Briggs* case later was credited as a primary influence in the *Brown* ruling. – *LS*

107

The summer of 1955 saw the first African American Little League in the state

All but one of the 61 chartered Little League programs in South Carolina was made up entirely of white players in the summer of 1955. The exception was the Cannon Street YMCA. Little League, the All-Stars, from Charleston, which was established two years earlier and became the first and only African American Little League team in South Carolina sanctioned by Little League Baseball, Inc. The league consisted of four teams sponsored by Black businesses and civic organizations and sustained by support from parents and the community. Though the league never gave the team the chance to compete at the Little League World Series, the All-Stars received recognition despite their dashed championship dreams and were inducted into Charleston's Baseball Hall of Fame. – *SB*

108

King spoke three times in Charleston

The Rev. Martin Luther King Jr. spoke on at least three occasions in Charleston, including remarks he gave at St. Matthew's Baptist Church and Emanuel AME Church in April 1962. Five years later on July 30, he spoke at Charleston County Hall, where he met local activist Esau Jenkins. Both men were featured on a recording of the event by journalist Eugene B. Sloan. The recording included a speech by King. It later sold in 2019 for $68,000. – *LS*

109

Emanuel AME Church and the civil rights movement

Emanuel African Methodist Episcopal Church on Calhoun Street in downtown Charleston gained modern-day notoriety in 2015 for the horrific racially-motivated attack that killed nine people, including senior pastor and S.C. Sen. Clementa Pinckney, and injured three others. But decades earlier, the historic church known as "Mother Emanuel," was a key location in the civil rights movement, hosting notable African American leaders such as Booker T. Washington, Dr. Martin Luther King Jr. and the Rev. Wyatt T. Walker. In the 1950s and 1960s, the Rev. B.J. Glover led the church. He was later the head of both Charleston and Columbia branches of the NAACP. Today, the church is listed on the U.S. Civil Rights Trail. – *LS*

110

First schools in state to desegregate

The city of Charleston's School District 20 was the first district in the state to desegregate. As the result of a court order, 11 Black children entered previously all-white schools in August 1963. It took eight years until the majority of public schools in the state integrated. – *LS*

111

1969 strike of Charleston hospital workers wins concessions

After the Medical College Hospital for the state of South Carolina fired 12 Black employees as they tried to unionize in March 1969, about 60 mostly female Black workers went on strike. The practical nurses, laundry workers, orderlies and others demanded the hospital reinstate their coworkers and recognize their union. Amid the protests, Coretta Scott King told more than 3,000 supporters that her late husband would have been there if he were alive. The strike lasted more than 100 days, and included mass demonstrations and arrests. Gov. Robert McNair declared a state of emergency for the city May 1. The workers won the reinstatement of their colleagues, but not the recognition of their union, Local 1199B. The hospital is now Medical University of South Carolina. – *LS*

112

Mary Moultrie begins organizing at Charleston Hospital strike

Mary Moultrie of Charleston was one of the women who led the strike at the Medical College Hospital in 1969. Arrested during the demonstrations, she is remembered for directly confronting Gov. Robert McNair in a speech, saying: "Unless you shape up, governor, our talking might just get a little bit louder. And our walking might just get a little bit longer." Moultrie served as founding president of Local 1199B of the Hospital and Health Care Workers' Union. In the early 2000s, Moultrie continued her organizing work by helping Charleston sanitation workers get better wages and working conditions. She was awarded a Harvey Gantt Triumph Award by YMCA of Greater Charleston in 2011 for her strike leadership and her work in human rights. Moultrie died April 27, 2015. – *LS*

113

Naomi White's "Hell's Angels" keep the night watch

Naomi White worked at Medical College Hospital in 1969 and went on strike with the other mostly Black women. She was arrested twice for her participation and is best known for her organization of the nighttime watch group called "Hell's Angels" that patrolled the neighborhood around the hospital and stopped employees attempting to cross the picket line. The group also enforced an economic boycott on shopping on King Street during the strike. – *LS*

114

Fielding becomes first Black elected to post-Reconstruction legislature

In 1970, Charleston businessman Herbert U. Fielding became the first African American elected to the S.C. General Assembly since Reconstruction, almost 100 years earlier. A Democrat who ran a successful funeral home, Fielding was active throughout the civil rights era, often paying bail for civil rights activists. "He was the main bridge that allowed Black and white people to come and engage and make progress together in the '60s and early '70s," former Charleston Mayor Joseph P. Riley said in 2015. Fielding served in the S.C. House of Representatives until 1984 when he was elected to the S.C. Senate. In 1992 after a failed bid for Congress, he returned to the family funeral business, Fielding Home for Funerals, started by his father in 1912. Fielding died at the age of 92 in 2015. – *LS*

115

"African American Flag" flies on America Street

An American flag in black, red and green has flown for nearly 30 years on a pole at America and Reid streets in Charleston's East Side, part of an exhibit from the 1991 Spoleto Festival USA. Nearby is a billboard of school children looking up toward the flag, which reflected the colors of Africa. Designed by Harlem-based artist David Hammons, it is called "African American Flag" and is a symbol of Black pride. It has remained controversial since its installation. Hammons printed five flags, one of which sold for $2.05 million in 2017. The flag and billboard are next to "The House of the Future," Hammons' take on the skinny houses of Charleston and a symbol of collective solidarity for the East side neighborhood. The property is now maintained by the city of Charleston. – *LS*

116

Charleston lawmakers lead on taking down Confederate flag, protecting monuments

Charleston state senators Robert Ford and Glenn McConnell, under pressure in 2000 from an NAACP boycott of the state, brokered a deal in the General Assembly to have four Confederate battle flags removed from inside and atop the Statehouse dome in Columbia. Ford, a Black Democrat, was the sole sponsor of what would become the Heritage Act, which protected Confederate and African American monuments alike. The act called for a two-thirds vote of both chambers of the General Assembly to modify or remove any monument or memorial on public land. The Confederate flag was moved to the Statehouse lawn, where it remained until 2015. After the racist attack at Emanuel AME Church that left nine people dead, including its pastor—S.C. Sen. Clementa Pinckney—the General Assembly voted to move the flag off the Statehouse grounds. – *LS*

117

Charleston offers a remarkable story of forgiveness

Though the tragic murder of nine worshippers at Mother Emanuel AME Church by a white nationalist gunman in 2015 is still fresh in the minds of Charlestonians, the words of those who lost loved ones are fresher still. Their words were heard around the word with comments such as "I forgive you" and "May God have mercy on you." Others said, "Hate won't win." Despite the hurt and anger, a powder keg of resentment that had grown in other communities didn't explode in Charleston following the murders. – *SB*

118

A president unites by singing "Amazing Grace" in Charleston

Nine days after a white nationalist killed nine members of Emanuel AME Church in a 2015 shooting that shocked the nation, President Barack Obama helped Charleston and the country heal. During a 40-minute eulogy of the church's pastor, state Sen. and the Rev. Clementa Pinckney, Obama led more than 5,500 people in an emotional singing of the hymn, "Amazing Grace." In the eulogy, he said, "Maybe we now realize the way racial bias can infect us even when we don't realize it. For too long, we've been blind to the unique mayhem that gun violence inflicts on this nation. It would be a betrayal of everything Reverend Pinckney stood for if we allow ourselves to slip into a comfortable silence again." – *AB*

119

Millions raised for International African American Museum

Former Charleston Mayor Joseph P. Riley Jr. initiated the idea for the International African American Museum, a museum under construction on the Cooper River where a wharf once stood as the first dry land in America felt by tens of thousands of enslaved Africans. Founders of the museum raised more than $100 million from public and private sources. At its groundbreaking ceremony in October 2019, many discussed the goal of finally getting African American history right after all this time. IAAM board chairman Wilbur Powers reportedly said, "That is a monumental task, but it's an important task, and we're committed to it." – *SB*

120

Black Lives Matter finds its voice in Charleston

Black Lives Matter, a movement born nationwide in 2013, came directly to Charleston in April 2015 after a white North Charleston police officer shot and killed Walter Scott, an unarmed Black man. A passerby videotaped the tragedy, which led to a national outcry, protests and the conviction of Michael Slager. That June, an avowed white supremacist opened fire and killed nine in a prayer group at Emanuel AME Church, a historic Black Charleston church. Black Lives Matter protesters joined 20,000 people in what was dubbed a "unity march." After the extra-judicial killings of blacks in other parts of the nation in 2020, the movement and local voices urged policing changes and social reform. After early demonstrations devolved into rioting and looting along King Street, authorities issued more than 50 arrest warrants. A day after the looting, Charleston police made national headlines for arresting protester Gee Jordan as he pronounced his love for them but refused to leave when ordered. – *LS*

121

Charleston apologizes for role in slavery

Charleston City Council formally apologized in 2018 for the city's role in the slave trade before it ended in the early 19th century. It has been estimated that as many as 40 percent of enslaved people brought into the United States came through the port of Charleston. The 2018 apology was supported by Mayor John Tecklenburg, who said during the vote that Charleston, with its strong ties to the slave trade, had a reason to apologize for its role. The council's vote was held on Juneteenth (June 19), often recognized as the official 1865 end-date of slavery in the United States. The council's resolution passed 7-5, with those opposing it saying they couldn't apologize for something they weren't a part of. – *LS*

122

Calhoun monument dismantled in 2020

A statue of John C. Calhoun, a powerful antebellum United States senator and former vice president of the United States, loomed over Marion Square atop a 115-foot pedestal in downtown Charleston for 124 years. In June 2020 after national howls of systemic racism that erupted following the death of a Black man in Minneapolis, Charleston City Council unanimously voted to remove the statue. Charleston City Councilman Robert Mitchell said before voting to remove the statue: "Being a person that was out here for a long time in the civil rights movement, I know how the city of Charleston was all those times back in the '50s. None of us talked about heritage, we talked about peace, coming together – it wasn't that way. It didn't happen. Now is the time. We need to have some healing process. I don't think a statue is a place that is going to bring a healing process if we let it stay there." – *LS*

Charleston arts and culture

123

Gullah language and culture draws inspiration from African roots

The rich Gullah/Geechee culture developed in the Lowcountry from deep roots of western African culture from enslaved Africans who powered the growth of the plantation system. Some of the most prominent of these roots can be seen in the Gullah language, such as the word for peanut, "guber," derived from the KiKongo word "N'guba." Today, you might recognize the English word "goober" as a derivative. Also, the word "gumbo" comes from a word from the Umbundu language of Angola meaning okra. Gullah's African ties are also apparent in the stories they tell, like those of "Bruh Rabbit," which mimic West and Central African trickster tales about the clever rabbit, spider and tortoise. Congressman James E. Clyburn has strived to preserve the Gullah/Geechee culture, reintroducing bills like the Gullah/Geechee Cultural Heritage Act in the U.S. House of Representatives and sponsoring similar legislation. – *SB*

124

Gibbes Museum of Art connects the city's past to the contemporary art scene

The Lowcountry's Gibbes Museum of Art is home to the foremost collection of art incorporating the story of Charleston. When Charleston was financially and culturally on its knees, philanthropist James Gibbes left a bequest to the city in 1888 to build an art museum, hoping for the city to rise again. When it opened in 1905, the nation celebrated what Charleston had always understood: the power of art. The Gibbes believes that "when you open yourself to art, you open yourself to the world," and "in the presence of art, you have the opportunity to see inside someone's heart, mind and soul and feel what they felt." In an effort to show this, exhibitions are designed as an experimental platform for visitors to experience art in new ways and challenge established interpretations. – *SB*

125

The Charleston Renaissance led to a cultural boom in the Lowcountry

Between World Wars I and II, the city of Charleston experienced a boom in the arts as writers, architects, artists, musicians and historical preservationists came together to represent and improve the city. This "Charleston Renaissance" period was part of a greater interwar artistic movement known as the Southern Renaissance that swept through the region. Today, it is credited with helping to kickstart the city's tourism industry. – *SB*

126

Smith remembered as a catalyst for the Charleston Renaissance

Alice Ravenel Huger Smith, born 1876, was a native artist and lifelong resident of Charleston. While she was primarily self-taught, she is best remembered for her scenic views of Charleston streets and poetic marsh vistas that capture the mystical aura of the Lowcountry. Hoping to convey an essential idealized representation of her subjects, she painted almost exclusively in watercolor from 1924 on. She, along with her associates, Elizabeth O'Neill Verner, Alfred Hutty, and Anna Heyward Taylor, was at the center of Charleston's artistic reawakening during the early 20th century as a founding member of the Charleston Etcher's Club and the Southern States Art League, as well as being involved in the Historic Charleston Foundation, Carolina Art Association, and Music and Poetry Society. Her work can be found today in many notable collections, such as the Brooklyn Museum, the Ogden Museum of Southern Art and the de Young Fine Arts Museums of San Francisco. – *SB*

127

Painter, preservationist is a leader of rebirth of Charleston arts

Elizabeth O'Neill Verner was born in 1883 in Charleston, first studying art with Alice Ravenel Huger Smith and later enrolling at the Pennsylvania Academy of Fine Arts. In 1907, she married E. Pettigrew Verner; however, it wasn't until 1925 that she would become a professional artist and the sole supporter for her children. She became a white portraitist known for representing African-Americans, especially the city's flower vendors, and illustrated DuBose Heyward's 1925 novel, *Porgy.* She came to specialize in drawings of historic buildings in effort to preserve the history of the city from her studio and home at 38 Tradd St. Her work is held by the Metropolitan Museum of Art, the Smithsonian American Art Museum and others across southeastern America. South Carolina's highest arts award is named for her. – *SB*

128

Hutty shows "decay and decrepitude" in his art

Renowned artist Alfred Heber Hutty, a northerner, is closely identified with the Charleston Renaissance of the 1920s because he rarely idealized the city, choosing instead to show the "decay and decrepitude" around him with his impressionistic oil paintings of Charleston streetscapes. He also depicted live oaks draped with Spanish moss, dilapidated old buildings and animated African Americans. In 1919, Hutty discovered Charleston while looking for a warmer place to spend his winter months. He embraced Charleston's beauty and lifestyle and for the rest of his life, he alternated homes between summers in Woodstock, N.Y., and winters in Charleston. Today, Hutty's work can be found around the state and in the Library of Congress, with the largest collection owned by the Gibbes Museum of Art. – *SB*

129

Printmaker seen as one of the leading Charleston Renaissance artists

Anna Heyward Taylor was born in Columbia in 1879 as one of eight children of a surgeon who served in the Civil War in the Army of Northern Virginia. She received an education from the South Carolina College for Women and graduated in 1897 before traveling around Europe to study art between 1903 and 1917. She then served in the American Red Cross in France and Germany during World War I, returning to America and settling in Charleston in 1920. There, she became known for her prints highlighting life in the Lowcountry, including agricultural subjects both past and present, local fauna and flora, architecture, street scenes and the city's tradespeople. Alongside Alice Smith, Elizabeth O'Neill Verner and Alfred Hutty, Taylor is today considered one of the four leading artists of the Charleston Renaissance. – *SB*

130

Guggenheim collection first exhibited in Charleston

The Gibbes Museum of Art offered the first public exhibition of the Solomon Guggenheim collection now at the Guggenheim Museum in New York City. After successful mining magnate and industrialist Solomon R. Guggenheim retired in the 1920s and took up collecting art full-time, he and his wife bought a winter home in Charleston. In 1936 – and again in 1938 – he allowed some of his collection to be shown at the Gibbes, the South's oldest art museum. On display were works from artists like Kandinsky, Picasso, Modigliani, Bauer, Chagall and Leger.

Today, many of the works first shown publicly in Charleston are centerpieces of the Founding Collection at the Guggenheim Museum in New York. In late 2016, the Gibbes again welcomed art shown first in the 1930s in Realms of the Spirit, a retrospective "from the Guggenheim collection [that] emphasizes the timeless founding vision of the museum and the belief that non-objective art conveys the spiritual joy of creation." – *AB*

131

DuBose Heyward proves to be a man of many talents

While writer DuBose Heyward is known primarily for his work as a novelist, he composed the lyrics for *Porgy and Bess* with Ira Gershwin. Heyward wrote *Porgy*, the book on which the opera was based. George Gershwin, like his brother, also spent time with author Heyward in the Lowcountry while composing the classic score. – *HE*

132

Story of *Porgy and Bess* based on Charlestonians

Local African-American vegetable vendors like the man featured in DuBose Heyward's *Porgy* lived and sold their produce from "Cabbage Row," a degeneration of Church Street from antebellum prosperity into slum-like tenements. Cabbage Row, called "Catfish Row" in Heyward's work, featured a real-life Porgy, Samuel Smalls, a crippled man whose main mode of transportation was a goat-pulled cart. Heyward reportedly heard of Goat Cart Sam from a local newspaper article that detailed Small's arrest in March 1924 after he reportedly tried to shoot a woman on Romney Street. The police caught him only after the vendor and his goat led them on a chase down several downtown alleys. — *SB*

133

The Jazz Age dance got America up and moving

"The Charleston" became a popular Jazz Age dance after professional dancers adopted it in the 1923 Broadway musical *Runnin' Wild.* The dance, known for its fast tempos and quick foot motions, is often viewed as a symbol of the decade. With strong parallels to dances from Nigeria, Ghana and Trinidad, the dance has roots in an African American folk dance known throughout the South before the 1920s. "The Charleston" song in the musical, which turned the dance into a national craze, was fueled by a beat that composer James P. Johnson reportedly first heard from Charleston dockworkers. – *HE*

134

Largest professional theatre company in S.C.

Charleston Stage, South Carolina's largest professional theatre company, makes its residence at the historic Dock Street Theatre on State Street in the heart of downtown Charleston. The organization also has a 10,000-square-foot performance and work facility in West Ashley that opened in 2019. Charleston Stage offers a full season of plays and musicals that "light up the stage with stunning scenery, dazzling costumes and brilliant lights! Productions feature a resident professional acting company of over 100 professional actors, singers, dancers, guest designers, choreographers, scenic artists and technicians." – *AB*

135

Sweetgrass baskets are steeped in history

People of African descent are believed to have been making baskets for as long as they have lived in the Carolinas. The early history of coiled grass baskets can be compared to the meteoric rise of rice farming along the Southeast coast, as can its fall—partly at the hands of the American Civil War, according to the Historic Preservation Society. A gradual shift from "work baskets" to "show baskets," which began around Boone Hall Plantation in Mount Pleasant, meant a change in materials from bulrush to sweetgrass, and from saw palmetto to cabbage palm. As the craft boomed in 1929, with baskets being sold in local shops on King Street and wholesale department stores in New York, basket production soared, and the craftsmen began selling their own products roadside to reach their primary market directly, capitalizing on Charleston's growing number of tourists. – *SB*

136

Antiques Week draws international eyes to historic artifacts

Charleston's legacy of European and Asian influences can be seen in its unique architecture and decorative arts. Due to this heritage, and the still present remnants of the physical history of the city, Charleston attracts the attention of connoisseurs around the world during springtime's Antiques Week. The event was designated by former Mayor Joseph P. Riley Jr. week out of the year that includes four major philanthropic events: the Charleston International Antiques Show, the Charleston Arts and Antiques Forum, the Spring Festival of Houses and Gardens, and the Charleston Symphony Orchestra League Designer Show House. – *SB*

137

MOJA Arts Festival celebrates one-ness through African and Caribbean culture

Held each fall, the MOJA Arts Festival: A Celebration of African-American and Caribbean Arts began in 1983, drawing its name, MOJA, from the Swahili word meaning "one." The festival, produced and directed by the City of Charleston Office of Cultural Affairs along with a MOJA committee and advisory board, puts a spotlight on the contributions of African American and Caribbean cultures to the entire world, including visual arts, classical music, dance, gospel, jazz, poetry, R&B music, storytelling, theatre, children's activities, traditional crafts, ehtnic food and more. About half of the events during the MOJA Arts Festival are free of charge. – *SB*

138

Sounds of the Gullah Geechee people reach far and wide

Gullah Geechee musical traditions, which partially derive from the South Carolina coastline, have influenced many popular genres of music, including soul, gospel, and jazz. While it's origin is still unknown, many believe that "Kumbaya" came from the Gullah people. Gullah Geechee music derived from African traditions and evolved in the time of enslavement. – *HE*

139

James Jamerson takes Charleston grooves to Motown

Lowcountry native James Jamerson performed on several iconic Motown songs and albums, influencing generations of bassists. His bass playing was essential for some artists such as Marvin Gaye. Jamerson performed on Gaye's legendary album *What's Going On* and his chart-topping smash "Ain't No Mountain High Enough." – *HE*

140

Ranky Tanky gets its day in the sun

Gullah band Ranky Tanky became a surprise national hit in 2017 with the release of their self-titled debut album. Composed of several popular jazz artists from the Charleston area, the band performs modernized versions of Gullah songs and uses the cultural traditions of their ancestors to create original music. The band's popularity reached a high point in 2019, when Mayor John Tecklenburg declared Dec. 17 as Ranky Tanky Day. – *HE*

141

Pachelbel is canon in a Charleston church

German composer Charles Theodore Pachelbel relocated to Charleston in the 18th century, where he worked as an organist in St. Philip's Church. Charles Theodore was the son of Johann Pachelbel, the composer of the famous *Canon in D*. – *HE*

142

Venues a-plenty in the Holy City

Charleston's structure in the Colonial Era was perfect for public performances. Concerts were held in the city's council chamber and churches, which was monetarily fruitful for musicians. – *HE*

143

Charity turns a profit at the Jenkins Orphanage

The Jenkins Orphanage, a home for young Black orphans founded by Reverend Daniel Jenkins, formed their first marching band in 1892. The group of 11 or 12 boys were taught to read music and perform by a local musician, and they used the public spectacle to solicit donations. The money raised at some performances purportedly fed the orphans for a week. – *HE*

144

The Jenkins Orphanage finds the rhythm

After honing their craft, the band at the Jenkins Orphanage had high-energy performances in the streets of Charleston that centered on virtuosic solos and non-traditional harmonic structures. The band had stumbled on a sound that's now referred to as ragtime and jazz. – *HE*

145

Talented artists find their way after the Jenkins Orphanage

Several famous jazz artists cut their teeth at the Jenkins Orphanage, including guitarist Freddie Green, trumpeter William "Cat" Anderson, and trumpeter "Jabbo" Smith. Green would perform in Count Basie's band for years, becoming an influential jazz guitarist. – *HE*

146

Gaillard Center offers world-class performances

The Charleston Gaillard Center, one of the city's most prestigious performing arts venues, is named for the late Mayor Palmer Gaillard. The original Gaillard Center opened in 1968. A multi-million-dollar renovation and reconstruction of the building, fueled by a large gift by Charleston-born billionaire Martha Rivers Ingram, began in 2012 and was completed in 2015. In addition to serving as a principal venue for world-class performances by the Charleston Symphony, the Lowcountry Jazz Festival and Spoleto Festival USA, the Gaillard has hosted Lyle Lovett, Harry Connick Jr., the Nashville Ballet, Emanuel Ax, Keb' Mo' and Chick Corea. Its continuing community outreach efforts also provide rich arts education through curriculum-based workshops, classes, and summer camps available to schools at no charge. – *HE*

147

Spoleto Festival USA brings the world to the Lowcountry

Since the inception of Spoleto Festival USA in 1977, Charleston and her visitors have been treated to performers in a wide variety of visual art forms from around the world. The world-famous festival takes place for 17 days each spring at the end of May and beginning of June. Through the years, it has grown significantly in popularity, becoming an event that people travel to from around the world, thanks to its notable opera, musicals, classical, and jazz performers. In 2016, the festival had an estimated $42 million impact on the Charleston economy. – *HE*

148

Piccolo Spoleto gives Charlestonians another great arts festival

Two years after the Spoleto Festival began, the city of Charleston's Office of Cultural Affairs created a companion festival called Piccolo Spoleto to celebrate smaller and regional artists. Like its sister festival, Piccolo Spoleto hosts visual arts exhibits and plenty of musical performances in late May and early June – with some events at no cost and others at half the price. The office coordinates up to 500 events, presentations, performances and more during the busy Piccolo Spoleto season. – *HE*

149

Shovels & Rope make music a family business

Shovels & Rope, the husband-and-wife Americana duo of Michael Trent and Carrie Ann Hearst, met and live in Charleston. The couple performed in the backing bands for each other's solo projects before dedicating themselves to Shovels & Rope at the beginning of the 2010s. – *HE*

150

High Water Festival floods Charleston with big acts

Shovels & Rope created the High Water Festival in 2017 after performing for about 10 years. The two-day indie, Americana and rock show generally takes place in spring. It has turned into a popular local event since its inception, thanks to performances from Charles Bradley, Grammy Award-winning Ranky Tanky and, of course, Shovels & Rope. – *HE*

151

Charleston shows Hospitality to the world

Indie band Hospitality landed on *Time*'s list of the 10 best songs of the 2010s decade for the single "I Miss Your Bones." The band's songwriter, Amber Papini, and drummer, Nathan Michel, are married and live in West Ashley, where they are music educators. The song was put on *Time*'s list alongside "Rolling in the Deep" and "Old Town Road." – *HE*

152

Hootie & the Blowfish explode onto the nation

Hootie & the Blowfish frontman Darius Rucker was born and raised in Charleston. The singer met the rest of his band in college at the University of South Carolina. Hootie & the Blowfish became megastars in the '90s thanks to the success of their 1994 LP *Cracked Rear View.* Rucker's baritone vocals on hits like "Only Wanna Be with You" is cited as one of the most iconic parts of the band's sound. – *HE*

153

Darius Rucker gets back to his roots

Charleston native Darius Rucker has paid tribute to the Holy City several times during his solo career. His 2010 album *Charleston, SC 1966* features a picture of him posing in front of the Arthur Ravenel Bridge. In 2015, the singer released "You Can Have Charleston," a song from his LP *Southern Style*. – *HE*

154

Author and advocate Jack McCray kept local jazz alive

Jack McCray was a popular jazz advocate and newspaper columnist in Charleston. His historical narrative, *Charleston Jazz*, defined the popular genre in the Lowcountry. He also helped to found Jazz Artists of Charleston and the Charleston Jazz Initiative. His death in 2011 at age 64 caught many by surprise, as described by singer Leah Suarez in the *Charleston City Paper:* "Jack McCray did not just stand for something. He lived for everything. He was a walking testament, quite literally, for 'carpe diem.' Jack knew how to have a grand time and make lasting relationships. He was genuinely human. He was a citizen of the world. He valued time, language, music, and the art of humanity. He worked to preserve history. He equally worked to create history. Jack was on a mission and, in many ways, I feel as though his mission had just begun." – *HE*

155

Jump, Little Children hops into the hearts of locals

Before the Charleston indie rock band Jump, Little Children went national, it was known around town for busking in the Market and energetic performances at the Dock Street Theatre. Even though the band originated in North Carolina, it became a Holy City fixture, often carving out time for special performances in Charleston near New Year's Eve. – *HE*

156

Jump has fans in high places

The fandom for Jump, Little Children is so rabid around the Lowcountry that U.S. Rep. Joe Cunningham, D-S.C., honored it in the *Congressional Record* on Dec. 10, 2019: "Jump has earned a substantial and loyal fan base that has followed them throughout the country, supporting their nine records and EPs, and literally thousands of energetic concerts that keep us showing up," he said. –*HE*

157

Tecklenburg reveals he's a Heineken man

Jazz piano player and Charleston Mayor John Tecklenburg in 1983 wrote and recorded a downbeat piano ballad, "Thank You, Mr. Heineken," about the kidnapping of the owner of Heineken. The song, released in 2013, is still on Spotify. Tecklenburg, an entrepreneur and former city economic developer, found a different calling in 2015. That's the year he was elected the first new mayor of Charleston in 40 years after the retirement of Joseph P. Riley Jr. – *HE*

CP

Buildings and architecture

158

The houses that are one room wide

The Charleston single house, found throughout historic Charleston and often replicated in suburban communities today, became the favored residential form in the city after the Fire of 1740. The typical house stands two stories or higher and is built on a rectangular plan with its narrow end facing the street. Chimneys are located in the rear of the house. Architectural historians have found most people built their homes in this style as a response to the hot and humid Lowcountry summers because the tall profile allowed for more air circulation. Many of these houses, some 2,000 of which can be found throughout the city today have side porches, or piazzas, that are slightly slanted to allow water to run off. Piazza ceilings may be painted light blue, mimicking the sky. Many older Charlestonians believe the color keeps mosquitoes away.– *CH*

159

Rainbow Row

Rainbow Row, one of the best known attractions in Charleston, refers to the vibrant pastel paint on the exteriors of buildings between 79 and 107 East Bay Street. Renovations on this stretch of homes started in 1931 with preservationist Dorothy Haskell Porcher Legge purchasing and renovating a house at 99-101 East Bay. She used bright colors associated with colonial Caribbean architecture as inspiration. As the buildings continued to be restored through the 1950s, the block in its entirety became known as Rainbow Row. – *CH*

160

Drayton Hall is early example of Palladian architecture

Drayton Hall (ca. 1747), located just 10 miles from downtown Charleston, is one of the earliest examples of Palladian architecture in the United States. Palladianism is based on the writings and buildings of humanist and theorist Andrea Palladio (1508-1580), who felt that architecture should be governed by reason and by the principles of classical antiquity. Drayton Hall has never been restored, so those who preserve it have the opportunity to study materials and designs from every period in the house's history. In 2018, Drayton Hall constructed the Sally Reahard Visitor Center, where visitors can view an orientation movie, the timeline of Drayton Hall and a collections exhibit. – *CH*

161

George Washington stayed in this Charleston home

The Heyward-Washington House was built in 1772 by Thomas Heyward, Jr., best known as one of four South Carolina signers of the Declaration of Independence. The "Washington" part of the name comes from George Washington's use of the home during his week-long stay in Charleston in May 1791. Built in the Georgian-style, the home features a collection of Charleston-made furniture including the Holmes Bookcase, a priceless piece considered one of the "finest examples of American-made colonial furniture," according to the Charleston Museum. The house is open for tours. – *CH*

162

How Charleston preserved its homes, character

The Preservation Society of Charleston, founded in 1920, recognizes, protects and advocates for the city's historic places. In its work today, the society often participates in public meetings where decisions affect Charleston's historic district and the city's built environment (a term that refers to all the physical parts of where we live and work). While the society reviews proposals for alterations, additions and demolitions as they apply to historic homes, it also advocates for smart growth in downtown Charleston, which is historically prone to flooding. – *CH*

163

First revolving fund to buy, restore historic properties

Like its sister preservation society, the Historic Charleston Foundation is an advocacy organization with a mission to continue the work of historic preservation. The foundation emphasizes the importance of evolving beyond just saving historic buildings into an organization that also looks at the needs of modern society. Founded in 1947, the foundation became the first preservation group in the country to establish a revolving fund for the purchase and restoration of historic properties. – *CH*

164

Manigault House features fine example of "Adam" style

The neoclassical Adam or Adamesque-style of architecture (1780-1850) found in Charleston is named for three Scottish brothers, Robert, James and William Adam. According to the National Register, you can find the details of the Adam style in mantels, doors and window mouldings. Charleston's Manigault House, which was designed by Gabriel Manigault for his brother Joseph, is influenced in part by Gabriel's studies in Geneva and London before the American Revolution. It features a bowed piazza, offset wide porches and wooden columns and is considered one of the finest examples of the Adam style in America. – *CH*

165

Spiral staircase is highlight of neoclassical home

Built in 1803, the Joseph Manigault House, located at 350 Meeting St., was the home of wealthy rice planters and merchants during the 18th century. The Charleston Museum has preserved the home since 1933, maintaining the integrity of the house's "Adamesque" style, a neoclassical style of building. The home today features the original spiral staircase in its impressive central hall, as well as historic pieces from the Charleston Museum's collections, including American, English and French furniture. – *CH*

166

The Grimke Sisters

In 1794, John F. Grimke purchased the Heyward-Washington house. While John, a Revolutionary War officer and long-standing justice of South Carolina's Court of Common Pleas and General Sessions, was an interesting figure in his own right, his daughters made history. Sarah and Angelina Grimke, also known as the Grimke sisters, were famous abolitionists and suffragettes. After growing up in Charleston, the pair converted to Quakerism and moved to Philadelphia, where they implored their Southern sisters to embrace the antislavery cause, as outlined in Angelina's 1836 *Appeal to the Christian Women of the South*. – *CH*

167

What you see is what they found

The Aiken-Rhett House was built in 1820 by merchant John Robison and later expanded by Gov. and Mrs. William Aiken, Jr. in the 1830s and again in the 1850s. The Historic Charleston Foundation acquired the house in 1995 and has preserved it "as found," meaning the organization has not altered the furniture, architecture or finishes, which date to the mid-19th century. Perhaps the most significant aspect of the Aiken-Rhett House is this very "as found" existence because it is one of the few urban, historic Charleston homes that still has its original slave quarters intact. The quarters have been virtually untouched since the 1850s, allowing visitors the opportunity to see how enslaved Africans lived in Charleston. – *CH*

168

Marion Square: From fortification to farmers markets

Today the home of downtown Charleston's popular Saturday morning farmers market and a popular gathering spot, Marion Square was once the location of defensive fortifications. By the late 1700s, the 10-acre property was transferred to the Charleston city government. In the 1840s, the site served as the green of Citadel College until the school was relocated to the city's west side. The name of the site was then changed to Marion Square, honoring Revolutionary War officer Francis Marion, and the ownership of the property was transferred to the Washington Light Infantry and the Sumter Guards, which played a pivotal role in Marion Square's preservation in the 1940s—preventing it from becoming a parking lot. – *CH*

169

Controversial monument removed in June 2020

John C. Calhoun (1782-1850) served as a congressman, secretary of war, vice president and United States senator from South Carolina. He was known for pushing the political theory of nullification, which held that states could "nullify" federal law. A hero to later Confederates, a statue of Calhoun on a 48-foot pedestal was erected in 1887, but was mocked, vandalized and sold for scrap. At the time, the African-American community viewed the monument as a symbol of Black oppression and Jim Crow segregation. In 1896, a bronze statue of Calhoun went atop a 115-foot marble pedestal in Marion Square. More than a century later, the City of Charleston erected a marker at the site explaining the context of the monument, which to many served as a reminder of white superiority and slavery. By 2020, as the country wrestled with systemic racism, demands for the statue to be removed surfaced, leading city leaders in June to vote to take it down. – *CH and SB*

170

From grand house to pumping station to festival headquarters

The Middleton-Pinckney House at 14 George St. is the headquarters of the renowned international arts festival, Spoleto Festival USA. In the late 18th century, though, the house was home to Frances Motte Middleton and her husband, John Middleton. Later, after John passed away, it was home to Frances and her new husband, Thomas Pinckney. The home, alternately known as the Elliot Mansion, was purchased by the city's Water Works Department in the late 1800s and served as office space, a pumping station and a collecting reservoir. It housed the Commissioners of Public Works until 1985. – *CH*

171

Early days of city water

The early days of Charleston saw settlers and, later, proper Charlestonians drinking water from shallow wells and rainwater collected in cisterns. Inevitably, poor sanitation practices contaminated these wells, forcing city leaders to look for a cleaner source of water. The Charleston City Council commissioned the construction of an artesian well at Meeting and Wentworth streets in 1823. Unfortunately, the 1,260-foot well only produced a small amount of water. Another attempted well in 1879 yielded 700,000 gallons per day, which led to the Council's granting a franchise to the City of Charleston Water Works Co. to develop a public water system, one of the country's first. – *CH*

172

Crossing the pond for flooding solutions

Preservation societies, citizens and local government officials today are working to curb increasing flooding in the city. In 2019, the City of Charleston and the Historic Charleston Foundation implemented the Dutch Dialogues, a planning and discussion program designed to spotlight the Dutch methodology for managing water and flood infrastructure. A final report on the Dialogues detailed new and innovative strategies to combat flooding, such as the leveraging of nature with tree planting campaigns, updating building codes and embracing policy changes. – *CH*

173

White Point Garden, a.k.a. Oyster Point, offers stunning views

One of the most iconic and photographed parks in downtown Charleston, White Point Garden offers stunning views of Fort Sumter and the Charleston harbor. Dotted with old oak trees, the garden is also home to the Williams Music Pavilion – a gazebo-like bandstand – and a display of Civil War cannons, even though none of them could have fired upon Fort Sumter (that was from Fort Johnson in 1861) The garden area was once called Oyster Point, named for the abundance of sun-bleached oyster shells that covered the ground. In 2007, a statue of Maj. Gen. William Moultrie was unveiled in the park on Carolina Day, which commemorates the patriot victory at Fort Sullivan in 1776 just days before the Declaration of Independence was issued. – *CH*

174

St. Philip's Church inters famous South Carolinians

St. Philip's Church was the first English church established in South Carolina. Built in 1733, the original building burned in 1835, but members replaced it with a similar structure that was completed in 1838. The church, located on aptly named Church Street, features a triple Tuscan portico, a prominent steeple, and at one time, a clock that played music at three intervals every day. When the Civil War started, the church donated its bells to the Confederate government to be cast into cannons. During the war, the church was hit 10 times by Union cannonballs, damaging the roof and organ. Designated a National Historic Landmark in 1973, the church was restored in 1993 and still has an active congregation. Its cemetery includes graves of famous South Carolinians, from John C. Calhoun to Charles Pinckney to Edward Rutledge. – *CH*

175

First theater saved during Depression

Charleston was home to one of the colonies' earliest theaters in 1736. Fronting Dock Street (now Queen Street), the theater did not last long, eventually becoming the Planters Hotel in 1809. The hotel prospered until the 1930s when it was abandoned and left in bad condition. In 1935, Charleston was admitted to the Federal Emergency Relief Administration's "historical program," and the former site of Planters Hotel was chosen for restoration. Under the guidance of architect Douglas D. Ellington, the building re-emerged as a theater, celebrating its grand re-opening in 1937. – *CH*

176

Philip Simmons, creator of beautiful iron gates

Blacksmith Philip Simmons was born on Daniel Island in a Gullah-speaking community in 1912. After moving to the peninsula in 1925, he became the apprentice of an elderly African-American wheelwright, Peter Simmons. Under Peter, Philip began a successful career as a blacksmith who could shoe horses, repair wagons, and make and mend tools – and who could also create beautiful decorative wrought-iron gates and balconies. Once he put all of his energy into the artistic branch of blacksmithing, Philip excelled, creating elaborate ironworks for grand homes south of Broad Street. In 1982, the National Museum of American History acquired a piece by Simmons. That same year, the National Endowment for the Arts, still in its infancy, welcomed Simmons in its initial class of fellows. Simmons, for whom a high school is named on Daniel Island, died in 2009. – *CH*

177

Garden dedicated to master ironworker

St. John's Reformed Episcopal Church bought and restored an 1850 stuccoed brick Gothic Revival structure in 1971 that first served as the Anson Street Chapel for African American Presbyterians and later was the St. Joseph's Roman Catholic Church. Twenty years later, in 1991, the church garden, the entry of which is marked by the "Heart Gate," was dedicated to well-known parishioner and master ironworker Philip Simmons, who designed the gate. – *SB*

178

Where to see some of Simmons's great work

Blacksmith Philip Simmons crafted more than 500 pieces of wrought iron throughout his long career. You can see examples of his work all over the Holy City. Some examples:

- Cross and egret gate, 2 St. Michael's Alley
- Double lyre gate, 5 Stoll's Alley
- Heart gate, 91 Anson St.
- Lyre gate, 65 Alexander St.
- Snake gate, 329 East Bay St.
- Tulip gate, 2 Stoll's Alley
- Visitor Center gate, 23 Meeting St.

– AB

179

Hotel features prominent artists' work

The Omni at Charleston Place opened in 1986 as the cornerstone of an economic revival project to jumpstart downtown Charleston. The hotel was built to mimic the 1800s-style buildings in the surrounding area. In 1995, Orient-Express Hotels Ltd. invested in and started operating the hotel as Charleston Place. Nine years later, the owner updated the name to Belmond Charleston Place, under which the luxury hotel operates today. The hotel displays art from prominent and local artists, such as the stenciled wood floors from Karl Beckwith Smith III. The 9-foot bronze horses of the "Quadriga" sculpture in the fountain at the front entrance by John W. Mills represent the significance of the horse in Charleston's history, as well as its present-day role. *– SB*

180

Archdale Street's Unitarian Church is the oldest of its kind in the South

The construction of the Unitarian Universalist Church on Archdale Street began in 1772, but was interrupted by the American Revolution. Sources say the British stabled horses in the unfinished building. Though the structure was originally built to house the overflow of the Independent or Congregational church on Meeting Street, the congregation was rechartered as the Unitarian Church of Charleston in 1839, making it the oldest Unitarian Church in the South. – *SB*

181

Robert Mills: Favorite son who becomes early architectural guru

Robert Mills (1781-1855), an architect from Charleston, was an early American celebrity who became an antebellum household name across the new republic. Mills defined his ambitions in a letter to Thomas Jefferson in 1808, declaring his desire to pursue "the honour and benefit of [his] country." As a result, his architectural designs and engineering projects reformed American architecture as a whole through the use of new construction techniques and rationalist thought inspired by Jefferson. Mills incorporated his idea of a progressive nation, expanded commerce and communication by using a blend of colonial Georgian and rational antiquarian styles. Some Mills-designed projects in Charleston include the Fireproof Building and a congregational church. Nationally, he is known for designing the Washington Monument, the U.S. Treasury Building, and other federal buildings in Washington, D.C. – *SB*

182

Ravenel Bridge opens in 2005

Travelers between Charleston and Mount Pleasant were able to use a bridge starting in 1929 with the opening of the John P. Grace Memorial Bridge. By 1966, the state built a second, wider bridge to accommodate more traffic, the Silas N. Pearman Bridge. Both were retired and demolished as part of the construction in 2005 of the third longest cable-stayed bridge in the western hemisphere, an eight-laned bridge named for former U.S. Rep. Arthur Ravenel Jr. of Charleston. – *SB*

183

Graveyards in the South were built differently from the North

Many Southerners, following a traditional English custom, interred their dead through the years in churchyards or family burial grounds. Though Charleston did have an "Old Burying Ground" around Magazine, Logan and Queen streets, no aboveground evidence of this site has survived over time, while most church graveyards of Charleston remain. Some of the earliest Charleston religious sites, such as the French Huguenot Church, the Circular Congregational Church, First Baptist Church of Charleston, St. Philip's Church, St. Michael's Church, St. John's Lutheran Church of Charleston, First Scots Presbyterian Church and the Unitarian Church in Charleston are still committed to preserving their historical graveyards. – *SB*

184

Spring Festival of Houses and Gardens blooms

Charleston's annual Spring Festival of Houses and Gardens, organized by the Historic Charleston Foundation, has been held during the peak of the city's blooming season, bridging March and April each year since 1947. The festival gives visitors the chance to go inside private residential interiors and gardens of about 150 of the country's most iconic historic houses in roughly a dozen colonial and antebellum neighborhoods. While guests enjoy the unique beauty of Charleston's architecture and gardens, the proceeds support the foundation's preservation mission to protect the history and culture of Charleston. – *SB*

CP

ARIAIL ©2020
NATHALIE DUPREE'S PORK CHOP THEORY
MAKE SURE YOUR PORK CHOP'S NOT LONELY...

Food

185

Nathalie Dupree, Charleston's own culinary celebrity

Nathalie Dupree is a best-selling author, James Beard Award winner, television star, and spunky, no-nonsense chef. She and historian husband Jack Bass live in downtown Charleston. Her many recipes (she's authored 15 cookbooks) play homage to the ingredients and techniques of the South. She's a founding chairman of the Charleston Wine + Food festival, a Grande Dame of the international organization Les Dames d'Escoffier, and a founder of Southern Foodways Alliance. Even with fame and acclaim, Dupree's common-sense culinary advice for the home cook is smartly simple. Good biscuits, for example, can be made with just two ingredients: cream and flour. For Thanksgiving, Dupree has said she cooks one turkey the night before, as well as her famed mashed potatoes. "Reheating in the microwave is perfectly acceptable." – *MSH*

186

Charleston is food oasis for James Beard Foundation

More than 30 Charleston-area chefs, restaurants, programs and culinary classics have won or been nominated for prestigious awards from the James Beard Foundation. Each year, the awards, often referred to as the "Oscars of the food world," recognize and celebrate chefs and culinary leaders who are making "America's food culture more delicious, diverse, and sustainable for everyone." Past semi-finalists and winners include Steve Palmer (restaurateur), FIG (restaurant), Mike Lata (chef), Rodney Scott (chef), Peninsula Grill (restaurant), Hominy Grill (restaurant), Cynthia Wong (pastry chef), Edmund's Oast (restaurant), Jason Stanhope (chef), Sean Brock (chef), David Howard (restaurateur), Ann Marshall (spirits), Alex Lira (chef) and Lauren Mitterer (chef). Two restaurants, Bertha's Kitchen and Bowen's Island Restaurant, have been named America's Classics by the foundation. – *MSH*

187

Charleston Wine + Food Festival enhances culinary reputation

This four-day culinary celebration founded in 2006 is held on the first weekend of March. Annually, it attracts about 18,000 visitors, about 58 percent of whom come from within 50 miles of the city. Considered one of the top five food and wine festivals in the country by *Forbes Travel Guide*, the event puts a spotlight on the talents of some of the region's and world's most celebrated chefs, culinary professionals and winemakers at more than 50 events that benefit local culinary charities and scholarships. Not to mention, it's fun – with events like the Waffle House Breakfast Throwdown and beverage tastings for kids, there's something for everyone. – *SB*

188

Lowcountry offers a briny delicacy with its oysters

Connoisseurs of oysters often believe the salty just-right-sized clusters hammered from the marshes of the Lowcountry are among the world's best. Culinary wizards Matt and Ted Lee say they're the flavor of the Lowcountry, describing roasting oysters over a wood fire as the quintessential Charleston experience — "the outdoor, rustic-as-heck, shuck-your-own roast is the thing, and it says a lot about Charleston's paradoxes and contrasts that the same ease and grace will be brought to an oyster roast as to high holidays with family." Note: The Lowcountry Oyster Festival is every January. – *AB*

189

She-crab soup

Charleston is the birthplace of she-crab soup. "The seafood specialty was created by William Deas, butler of former Mayor R. Goodwyn Rhett. Mayor Rhett entertained President William H. Taft, who helped make the famous dish," according to Explore Charleston. Rhett reportedly wanted to impress the visiting Taft, who loved turtle soup. So Rhett asked Deas to add something special to his regular local crab soup. He reportedly spooned in crab roe. Taft loved it. And she-crab soup was born. (Recommendation: Add a little sherry to your bowl just before slurping down.) – *AB*

190

Hoppin' John is more than rice and peas

Hoppin' John means two things to Charlestonians. First, it's a rich mixture of two Lowcountry kitchen staples – rice and black-eyed peas – that reflects the region's culinary heritage, which stemmed from the pots and traditions of enslaved Africans. The dish is often flavored with spicy sausage, bacon, ham or pork fat, with some recipes adding onions, fresh tomatoes and seasonings. Residents of Charleston also know "Hoppin' John" to be a nickname for culinary writer and historian John Martin Taylor, who ran the culinary bookstore "Hoppin John's" in Charleston from 1986 to 1999. Taylor played a crucial role in educating people across the South about the importance of traditional Southern dishes and high-quality, authentic ingredients. Today, he operates an online store. – *AB*

191

Bowens Island Restaurant is a Lowcountry staple

In the old days of Bowens Island Restaurant, the bathrooms weren't anything to write home about. But people loved the food so much that they'd flock there anyway. After a fire a few years back led to a new building (with nice bathrooms), the restaurant with roots from 1946 has been going stronger than ever, even winning a James Beard Award for being an American classic. Initially only accessible by boat, owners May and Jimmy Bowen eventually built a narrow causeway from Folly Road across the marsh. After both died, their grandson, lawyer and divinity school graduate Robert Barber Jr., took over. The original building burned down in 2006, but Barber rebuilt it with a pavilion overlooking the scenic Folly River. Today, Bowens Island Restaurant is home to tantalizing fried shrimp, wood-roasted oysters, lightly-fried fresh fish, sweet hushpuppies and more. In fact, there's not much of a better authentic Lowcountry dining experience than the down-home goodness found in this joint. – *AB and MSH*

192

The Lowcountry's long history of oystering

In the past few years, those visiting the Holy City have been able to enjoy both "R" month oyster roasts and year-round singles at area raw bars and restaurants. The wild oyster population is not what it once was, though. From the late 1880s to just after World War II, the oyster industry had its heyday and was South Carolina's most valuable fishery – in 1902, oysters were responsible for 45 percent of the value of all South Carolina fisheries. From 1900 to 1935, oyster canneries grew in number, employing thousands of workers and processing most of the state's oysters to then be shipped to many parts of the world. The primary oyster industry centers were located in Bluffton, Beaufort, Port Royal, Folly Beach, Awendaw, and McClellanville. – *MSH*

193

Charleston's early restaurant scene included rival hotel dining rooms

Charleston, a city now known around the globe for its ever-evolving and impressive dining scene, began to explore the world of "haute cuisine" in the early 19th century. In the spring of 1838, three rival establishments – the Charleston Hotel, the Victoria Hotel, and the Planter's Hotel – competed for the best personnel and equipment, raising the stakes for hotel dining. Planter's renovated its kitchen, installing Dr. Nott's patented portable baker and boiler. The Charleston Hotel curated a fine *a la carte* menu to match its "superb saloon." The Victoria hired a talented caterer. – *MSH*

194

Most valued in the late-18th century kitchen? Pastry cooks

Skilled bakers were highly sought after during the late 18th and early 19th centuries, particularly those who could produce sweet and savory creations. This skill set even crossed race lines at the time as pastry cooks were among the most valuable of the city's enslaved men and women. The full title for those most highly regarded in this field was "complete pastry cook." After reportedly winning her freedom in 1795, Sally Seymour was able to open her own pastry shop on Tradd Street, training her children and an enslaved staff to "bolster her production." After her death, Seymour's daughter Eliza assumed control of the shop. Eliza and her husband John would go on to run four establishments: The Mansion House, the Lee House, the Jones Hotel, and the Moultrie House. – *MSH*

195

The legendary Nat Fuller hosts mixed-race dinner

Nat Fuller, a once enslaved Black butcher turned restaurant owner, may be best known for hosting the first mixed-race dinner in Charleston in the spring of 1865 at his restaurant, Bachelor's Retreat on 103 Church St. Enslaved from birth until the late 1820s, Fuller was trained as a cook by financier William C. Gatewood who wanted to entertain guests in his home. Fuller held a culinary apprenticeship under Eliza Seymour Lee (yes, the same Eliza of pastry fame above) in the 1820s, and became a major purveyor at the Charleston Game Market in the 1840s. He developed a successful mobile catering business, becoming the "most popular banquet provisioner" in the 1850s. He opened his own establishment – boasting a two-story brick kitchen and serving "breakfast, dinner, supper, lunch and oysters" – in the fall of 1860. Fuller died of typhoid fever in 1866. – *MSH*

196

Charleston's 18th century denizens ate beef, not turkey, for the holidays

While most modern Thanksgiving and Christmas meals involve some kind of large cooked bird, a nice cut of beef was just the thing in the 1700s for wealthy Charleston families. According to Drayton Hall's Wood Family Fellow Jenna Carlson, "calves' heads were often the fare of 18th century elite in both the Lowcountry and Chesapeake." Carlson reported that the wife of a planter, Harriott Pinckney Horry, included a recipe for dressing a calf's head in her recipe book. It called for "placing half of the head in the center of the platter and dressing it with a stewed concoction made with the other half of the head." Yummy? – *MSH*

197

The city's fish market was once woefully barren

From 1810 until the start of the Civil War, visitors to the Charleston Market reported there was a lack of stalls for fresh fish and seafood. During a tour of the Southern states after an 1826 visit to the market, the Duke of Saxe-Weimar-Eisenach reported: "Fish were not presented in so great a variety as I expected. Of shell fish, I saw oysters only ..." Larger fishing vessels (which caught the most marketable fish, sea bass) were primarily owned by Northerners, and the "mosquito fleet," which was locally manned by free blacks and Cubans, did not venture into the ocean, staying instead along the coastline. After emancipation, a huge new labor force was able to replenish the market with *fruits de mer*. – *MSH*

198

George Washington dined at McCrady's

Though McCrady's in Charleston has housed many concepts since being built in 1788 – a coffee house, a grocery, a wax museum – and entertained a variety of guests (both wanted and not)–it still stands at Unity Alley today. Unfortunately, it closed in 2020, victim of the coronavirus pandemic. Most recently a high-end tasting room, McCrady's first played host to society's gentlemen with elaborate dinners. On May 4, 1791, America's first president supped in fine fashion in the building's "Long Room," an 18th-century term for assembly hall. George Washington's dinner featured a whopping 30 courses, followed by 15 toasts, each "succeeded by a discharge from the field pieces of the Charleston Battalion of Artillery." Washington described the meal in his diary as a "sumptuous feast." – *MSH*

199

Charleston boasts North America's only working tea farm

The Charleston Tea Farm, located at 6617 Maybank Hwy. on Wadmalaw Island, is the only working North American tea farm. With sandy soil, a subtropical climate, and an average rainfall of 52 inches a year, the island provides the "perfect environment" for propagating tea. The farm's 127 acres produces nine different tea flavors; this is the only tea *in the world* made with 100 percent tea grown in America. The variety packs of Charleston Plantation tea can be purchased at most small markets and larger grocery chains. Charleston Tea Garden changed its name in 2020 from Charleston Tea Plantation. – *MSH*

200

A brief history of shrimp and grits

The celebrated dish on menus around the South got its start in Charleston as "shrimp and hominy," first seen in Blanche S. Rhett's 1930 cookbook *Two-Hundred Years of Charleston Cooking.* Rhett writes, "This is a delicious breakfast dish, served in almost every house in Charleston during the shrimp season." In 1951, the Junior League of Charleston's cookbook, *Charleston Receipts* published a "breakfast shrimp" recipe that had become more elaborate, resembling the dish we see today – Mrs. Ben Scott Whaley's recipe called for green pepper, bacon fat, onion, Worcestershire, ketchup, and flour to thicken. But Gaffney, S.C., native Bill Neal popularized the dish at his Chapel Hill, N.C. restaurant, Crook's Corner. A 1985 recipe in *The New York Times* launched the dish into the nation's collective conscience. Neal inspired chefs like John Currence and Robert Stehling, who has said his Hominy Grill shrimp and grits most resemble Neal's recipe. – *MSH*

201

How barbecue tasted in colonial times

Though there aren't many references to barbecue in the early days of the Carolinas, by the early 1770s, Charleston merchant William Richardson encountered his first taste of the low and slow cooking at a horse race in Camden, S.C. In a letter to his wife back home, Richardson wrote about his experience, which was apparently unlike anything he'd been privy to in Charleston: "I absolutely saw one lady devour a whole Hog head except the bones, don't tell this to any of your squeemish C Town ladies for they will not believe you, had some of them been near our feast & their appetites Gorged with what you in town call delicases (but what we Crackers dispise) they perhaps might think us cannibals & with some propriety they might think, if the could suppose a half rosted hog, with the blood running out at every cut of the Knife, any thing like human flesh but ye squeemish C Town ladies I would not have ye think our buxom Cracker wenches so degenerate!" – *MSH*

202

Carolina Gold rice

Gold rice, once central to Southern coastal cuisine, was barely in cultivation by the 1940s, supplanted by conveniently mass-produced long grain white rice. During the antebellum period, "planter-naturalists" described Gold Seed Rice as "an oblong grain 3/8ths of an inch in length, slightly flattened on two sides, of a deep yellow or golden color, awn short; when the husk and inner coat are removed, the grain presents a beautiful pearly-white appearance – an ellipsoid in figure, and somewhat translucent." Thanks to the USDA seed banks and agricultural pioneers like Glenn Roberts, Anna McClung, and the Carolina Gold Rice Foundation, the legendary grain is now available for modern mouths. Locally, Anson Mills now produces this grain (you can order some online for yourself), describing the product as "delicate, non-aromatic white rice with chameleon starch properties that allow it to produce fluffy, individual grains." The grain, when cooked properly, is creamier than any risotto or mashed potato, with a hint of sweetness. – *MSH*

203

Charlestonians have always loved to drink wine

Martha Zierden, curator of historical archaeology at the Charleston Museum, has uncovered archaeological proof over the years that Charlestonians have always been in good spirits. Literally. Excavations along the waterfront were "particularly loaded" with shards of green glass and remnants of heavy glass bases and hand-formed necks. Sealed wine bottles told an even greater tale of who was sipping: the museum's 2008 South Adger's Wharf dig produced a bottle with a "Laurens" seal, which Zierden says likely came from the cellar of wharf co-owner John Laurens. And as for the content of the bottle? Most likely Madeira wine, hailing from the Atlantic island of Madeira, "ideally situated for the trans-Atlantic trade." – *MSH*

204

Inside the kitchen of a signer of the Declaration of Independence

Built in 1772, the Heyward-Washington House is a Georgian style townhome once occupied by Thomas Heyward Jr., a signer of the Declaration of Independence. Today you can still tour the house, located at 87 Church St., and see its 18th-century kitchen building, constructed separate from the house to keep heat out of the house and reduce the danger of the house burning. Archaeological records of the site show glazed earthenware pots and pans were used, in addition to cast iron griddles, butter pots, milk pans, and pastry pans. Colonowares, a type of earthenware produced by African Americans along the Atlantic coast, were also used in these city kitchens. Other earthenware hailed from the Philadelphia region and England. – *MSH*

205

Charleston's Gullah cuisine offers more than red rice

Charleston is smack dab in the historic Gullah Geechee Corridor, which spans from North Carolina to Florida. This National Heritage Area has been designated by Congress as a place where "natural, cultural, and historic resources combine to form a cohesive, nationally important landscape." The foodways of the Gullah Geechee, intrinsic to Lowcountry history, started in West Africa. The Gullah Geechee people are descendants of Africans who were enslaved on the plantations growing rice, indigo, and Sea Island cotton. The enslavement on these isolated islands helped these men and women maintain and transform a distinct culture of food, art, music, and language. Today, those visiting the Holy City can eat true Gullah food at restaurants like Bertha's, Nana's, Martha Lou's, Hannibal's, and Ravenel Seafood. These establishments are known for dishes like fried shrimp, garlic crabs, red rice, fried chicken, baked macaroni, lima beans, and cornbread. – *MSH*

206

Fire puts an end to Charleston's colonial beef market

Charleston's "Beef Market" was constructed in 1760. Prior to this, cattle were slaughtered in a smaller, more "informal venue." Before the 1730s, cattle were slaughtered outside the city walls. The Broad St. Beef Market burned down in 1796 and was not rebuilt as the character of the street no longer allowed for a "low dirty-looking market for beef." In 1800, City Hall was constructed on the market's remains, sealing in troves of archaeological evidence of the times. When the Charleston Museum excavated the remains of the market in 2004, archaeologists recovered bones and ceramics dating back to the three market eras. Evidence gathered suggests that "the market was a vibrant public area, one used as a public gathering space where residents might visit and converse and perhaps share refreshment." That's reminiscent of the present-day Marion Square Farmers Market, perhaps – sans the slaughter of animals, of course. – *MSH*

207

Ducks, woodcocks, and tigers, oh my

As early as 1686, Huguenot Jean Boyd described the eating of "bear and tigers (wildcat), as well as stags and wild turkeys" in a letter to the Old World. He also listed "quantities of ducks, teal, wild geese, woodcocks, two or three types of snipe, sea larks and cormorant" as well as "very good rabbits and hares, and squirrels." Archaeological records show opossums were caught and, if captured alive, would be "cleaned out" by "feeding for several days on milk, bread, and potatoes." Yum? Beaver tails were considered a delicacy by some; otters were hunted primarily for their pelts; and bears were hunted for their fur, grease, and meat. – *MSH*

208

The taking of tea

Archaeological records from the 18th century tell us that tea time was for genteel denizens and the working class. Proper tea etiquette required "a retinue of new, specialized material items" beginning with the tea table. The table was set with a teapot (preferably silver or porcelain), plus a cream pot, sugar bowl, tongs, cups, saucers, and teaspoons. – *MSH*

CP

Charleston's economy

209

Top destination in U.S. for eighth year in a row

Readers of *Travel + Leisure* magazine in 2020 named Charleston as the top U.S. travel destination, a recognition it won for the eighth year in a row. The magazine also listed Charleston as the only U.S. destination in the reader survey of the world's top 20 destinations. According to the magazine, readers tapped Charleston for the top honor because of its blend of history, culture, architecture, hospitality and food. According to a press release, the magazine's editor-in-chief, Jacqui Gifford, said, "It's been exciting to watch the evolution of this uniquely American city, beloved by our readers for its welcoming spirit, nourishing, inventive food, and world-class cultural events. There's always something happening in Charleston—and you don't want to miss out on the party," she said in 2019. – *AB*

210

Tourism plows billions into local economy

One of the Charleston area's biggest economic drivers is tourism, according to Helen Hill, CEO of Explore Charleston, the new name for the Charleston Area Convention and Visitors Bureau. According to a College of Charleston analysis, tourism generated $8.13 billion in economic impact in 2018 and directly employs more than 40,000 people throughout the region. "A thriving visitor market enhances the quality of life for local residents through increased air service, vibrant cultural and entertainment amenities, as well as expanded dining and retail options," Hill said in a press release. "A stronger tax base generated by the hospitality and travel industries reduces the reliance on property taxes paid by local residents." – *AB*

211

Tourism becomes Charleston's largest industry

Charleston's Navy Yard and Naval Base closed in 1995 after nearly a century of operation. With humble beginnings as a drydock, the yard, more recently known as the Charleston Naval Shipyard, was a U.S. Navy shipbuilding and repair facility on the Cooper River in North Charleston. After its closure, a large chunk of Charleston's industrial side left with it, leaving a gap to be filled by the growing city's tourism industry for which it is now known. More than 7 million people now visit the Charleston area annually. – *SB*

212

The Great Fire of 1838

A large fire that damaged more than 1,000 buildings and claimed multiple lives began April 27, 1838, and raged until noon the next day. Charleston's Trinity Church and several churches were burned, the entire market except for the fish section was destroyed, and one-quarter of all businesses in the main part of the city were ruined. When people rebuilt after the fire, Charleston saw a surge in the Greek Revival architectural style, which is still seen today and makes Charleston an architectural destination. The Gothic Revival style with its picturesque forms and reminders of devout European religion also made an appearance in the construction of churches after the fire.– *LS*

213

The Great Fire of 1861

Two years before the Union bombardment of Charleston began and eight months after the first shots of the Civil War were fired at Fort Sumter, fire ravaged the city. The conflagration began Dec. 11, 1861, at the intersection of East Bay and Hasell streets. Fourteen houses on Queen Street were destroyed to create a fire block and save the Marine and Roper hospitals, the Medical College and the Roman Catholic Orphan House. The fire burned itself out by noon Dec. 12, 1861, after it had consumed 540 acres, 575 homes, five churches and numerous businesses. The fire is considered the worst in the city's history. – *LS*

214

1911 hurricane ruined what was left of Charleston's rice industry

Vast amounts of wealth were carried into Charleston on the backs of rice farmers, but by the 20th century, many of the rice fields and plantations were beginning to go under, thanks in part to the turmoil of the American Civil War. But the final straw came In 1911 when a hurricane hit the city and neighboring rice fields recorded wind speeds between 94 and 106 mph. It destroyed what remained of the once-booming rice industry in the state by contaminating the fields with saltwater. – *SB*

215

Sofa Super Store fire kills 9 firefighters

Nine Charleston firefighters died in the Sofa Super Store fire on June 18, 2007. It was the deadliest firefighter disaster in the United States since the Sept. 11, 2001 terrorist attacks on New York City until two deadly wildfires erupted in 2013. An investigation found the fire in the West Ashley section of Charleston began in some discarded furniture in the loading dock area, but a source of ignition was never determined. At least 16 firefighters were inside attempting to quash the fire when a flashover – a near-simultaneous ignition of combustible materials – occurred. The roof collapsed, trapping and killing nine: Louis Mulkey, Mike Benke, Melvin Champaign, William "Billy" Hutchinson, Bradford "Brad" Baity, James "Earl" Drayton, Mark Kelsey, Michael French and Brandon Thompson. The location of the former warehouse has been transformed into a memorial for the men who died. – *LS*

216

The exposition comes to Charleston

The city of Charleston hosted the only world's fair in the history of South Carolina from December 1901 to May 1902. The South Carolina Interstate and West Indian Exposition, also known as the Charleston Exposition, attracted 675,000 people to the Cotton Palace. The palace and many of the other structures built for the expo no longer stand. The only buildings that remain are a bandstand at Hampton Park and Lowndes Grove, which was the exposition's Women's building. The regional trade show was held on 250 acres of land that is now home to The Citadel and Hampton Park. Famous visitors during this time included President Theodore Roosevelt and inventor and businessman Thomas A. Edison, who took panoramic video of the expo, now available through the Library of Congress. – *LS*

217

Home to nation's fifth best city hotel

Readers of *Travel + Leisure* magazine rated The Spectator Hotel in Charleston as tied for being the fifth best city hotel in the country in 2019, noting that it "charms with 'incomparable service' and rooms that are 'quiet, stylish, comfortable, and luxurious.'" The 10 top hotels in Charleston in 2019, according to the magazine's readers, were: Top Charleston City Hotels for 2019: The Spectator Hotel, Wentworth Mansion, Zero George, The Vendue Hotel, John Rutledge House Inn, The Restoration Hotel, Planters Inn, The Dewberry, Belmond Charleston Place and the French Quarter Inn. – *AB*

218

Charleston County is bigger than Rhode Island

At 1,358 square miles, Charleston County is the largest county in the state by total land and water area. That's larger than the state of Rhode Island, which covers an area of 1,214 square miles. If you take out the 442 square miles of water, which includes meandering marshes and beautiful beaches, the county has 916 square miles of land stretching more than 100 miles from the South Santee River north of McClellanville to Edisto Island. – *AB*

219

MUSC is a Lowcountry economic engine

Powered by more than 14,000 care team members, faculty and staff, the Medical University of South Carolina is the largest non-federal employer in the Charleston area. It accounts for 12 percent of the Charleston area economy and is directly or indirectly responsible for one out of every 12 jobs. – *AB*

220

Charleston County is growing

The metropolitan Charleston area's growth has been explosive in recent years with a net of 26 people moving into the area each day of the year, according to the Charleston Regional Development Alliance. Growing an average of three times the national average, the Charleston area's growth from 2010 to 2018 was 18.5 percent, slightly higher than the 15.9 percent growth for Charleston County. As of July 2018, 405,905 people lived in Charleston County, while the three-county metro area reached almost 800,000 residents. – *AB*

221

City of Charleston continues to grow, too

The Lowcountry's traditional hub, the city of Charleston, has grown through the years, more than doubling since its 1980's population of 69,779 people. In 2018, the city had an estimated 136,208 residents, according to U.S. Census projections. Compare that to the city's population 200 years ago in 1820 when 24,780 people lived in the Holy City. – *AB*

222

Downtown condo set residential sales record

A penthouse condominium and rooftop terrace atop the People's Building on Broad Street broke an all-time Charleston residential sales record in March 2020 in a $12 million deal. Philanthropist Terri Henning decided to sell the residence atop the city's first "skyscraper," an eight-story building, in favor of rental property, according to *The Post and Courier.* The penthouse includes three bedrooms and 3.5 baths in more than 8,000 square feet plus a rooftop terrace of 3,200 square feet. The city's second-highest residential sale also occurred in 2020 when the 17,142-square-foot Sword Gate House on Legare Street sold for $10 million in July. Built in the early 1800s, it is one of the city's largest and most historically-significant private homes. – *AB*

223

Neighboring communities experience rapid growth

Just as Charleston has grown through the years, so have North Charleston and Mount Pleasant. North Charleston, an industrial powerhouse that is the third largest city in South Carolina, wasn't incorporated until 1972. With annexation, it grew to 62,479 people by 1980 and had 113,237 people by 2018. East of the Cooper River, the once sleepy village of Mount Pleasant has exploded into a suburban utopia for many. In 1880, it had 783 residents, which grew to 14,464 by 1980. But in 2018, the community had almost 90,000 residents, according to Census figures. – *AB*

224

Poverty is a drag on Charleston-area economy

While the Charleston metropolitan area's median household income for 2017 was just shy of the $60,336 national average, the region's poverty rate of 11.9 percent found more than 90,000 residents living at or below the federal poverty level. About half of residents were white and 42 percent were Black. But within racial groups, 19 percent of blacks and 27 percent of Hispanics lived in poverty in 2017, compared to 8 percent of white residents. – *AB*

225

Charleston business continues to grow

The value of all U.S. goods and services exported by Charleston businesses in 2017 was 11.3 percent of the Gross Regional Product, which was ranked third among peer metropolitan areas such as Raleigh, Austin, Richmond and Nashville. Charleston also ranked first among similar metro areas in the concentration of small- and medium-sized businesses with 67.1 employees per thousand. The area saw a 16 percent growth rate in small firms – five times the national rate. – *AB*

226

Airport passengers soared in 2019

Charleston International Airport, served in 2019 by eight airlines, continued to soar with 5.6 passengers per capita in 2018, a marker of a strong economy. The Charleston airport's 4.3 million passengers in 2018 made it have the fastest growth among peer metro areas, such as Jacksonville, Seattle, Salt Lake City and Greenville, S.C. Passengers flying in and out of Charleston dropped precipitously in the spring of 2020 thanks to the coronavirus pandemic, but they slowly started returning by summer. – *AB*

227

The Lowcountry's port shares the wealth

Charleston's port and the inland ports connected to it account for more than 10 percent of South Carolina's annual economy, generating an economic impact of $7.8 billion, creating nearly 28,000 jobs, and spreading its wealth to neighboring states across the Southeast. – *SB*

228

The number of visitors to Charleston is staggering

Hailed as one of the best travel destinations in the world by different magazines and travel guides, it's no surprise to learn that Charleston welcomes more than 7 million visitors each year. Their impact supports more than 47,000 jobs with their economic impact on the area. – *SB*

229

Charleston's Boeing plant takes flight

Boeing's South Carolina manufacturing facility in North Charleston opened in 2011, becoming the company's first 100 percent renewable energy site, with up to 20 percent of that energy being supplied by more than 18,000 solar panels installed on the roof of the 787 Final Assembly building. The plant employs more than 7,000 South Carolinians, making it an economic powerhouse for the state. – *SB*

230

Volvo revs up production in South Carolina

Breaking ground in 2015 and starting production in 2016, Volvo's Berkeley County production site was seeing 150,000 cars rolling off the line annually, with its American-made S60s being exported around the world through the Port of Charleston. Prior to the COVID-19 pandemic, Volvo was estimated to generate about $5 billion in economic activity in South Carolina and support around 9,000 jobs by 2020. – *SB*

231

Silicon Harbor may be a household name in the near future

Shane Snow, a tech junkie, entrepreneur and New York-based journalist, dubbed Charleston as Silicon Harbor in a 2012 article, borrowing a phrase coined by PeopleMatter CEO Nate DaPore. Though many cities throughout the country have called themselves Silicon-something, Snow said Charleston deserves it for the vast number of people here trying to do innovative things and its designation as one of the top 10 fastest-growing cities for software and internet technology. – *SB*

CP

ARIAIL©2020
HOLLINGS WAS RIGHT - THERE'S NO EDUCATION IN THE SECOND KICK OF A MULE ... OR THE THIRD... OR THE FOURTH ... OR...
A
CITADEL
CITADEL v. ARMY
7 LOSSES 2 WINS

Education

232

New school colors set colleges apart

The College of Charleston's original "spirit colors" were light blue and white, but were changed in the early 20th century when its athletic program began competing against The Citadel because it had the same colors. Today's CofC athletic colors are maroon, gold and gray. – *AB*

233

Oldest—and newest—law school established

In November 1825, a group of Charleston attorneys were granted a charter by the State of South Carolina to establish a "Lecture-ship on the Law." In February 1826, The Forensic Club began offering lectures in the law, thereby laying the foundation for what essentially was the South's earliest law school. In 2004, the Charleston School of Law opened and, as a tribute to the first Forensic Club, re-established the club as a special honorary society for top graduates who demonstrated significant leadership, professionalism, public service and academic commitment. That's how the oldest law school in the South can also be the newest one in the state! – *AB*

234

American College of the Building Arts has unique education model

The American College of the Building Arts, founded in the aftermath of Hurricane Hugo to train much-needed skilled artisans to maintain historic buildings, started recruiting students in 2004, awarding its first college degrees five years later. "The college's model is unique in the United States, with its focus on total integration of a liberal arts and science education and the traditional building arts skills," according to Wikipedia. A four-year liberal arts and science college in Charleston, it offers craft specializations in six areas – blacksmithing, carpentry, classical architecture, plaster, stone carving and timber framing. – *AB*

235

Burke was city's only Black public high school for years

Burke High School got its start in 1910 as the first public high school for African Americans in the city of Charleston. The school, then known as the Charleston Colored & Industrial School, opened with 375 students in 1911. Ten years later, it was renamed Burke Industrial School to honor J.E. Burke, vice chairman of the public school board. The school had 1,000 students by 1930, including a full elementary, vocational and high school curriculum. By the end of World War II, Burke far exceeded its capacity. In 1954, when it merged with Avery High School, it was renamed Burke High School and had 2,000 students. Burke's students later took an active role during the civil rights movement by staging sit-ins at the lunch counters of Woolworth's and Kress on King Street, which led to the arrests of 24 students. In 1993, Burke became the first school in the state to have a campus-based health clinic. The school was rebuilt in 2005. – *AB and SB*

236

Citadel, College of Charleston offer more than 200 majors, minors

The College of Charleston offers more than 60 major degree programs including traditional tracks and others less familiar, such as computing in the arts, exercise science, historic preservation and community planning, meteorology and supply chain management. Among the 83 minor programs are classics, coaching, entrepreneurship, geoinformatics, global trade, Southern studies, and writing, rhetoric and publication. The Citadel offers 28 cadet majors, including cyber operations, intelligence and security studies, nursing and sports management. Among its 40 minors are East Asian studies, international criminal justice, leadership studies, non-Western studies, sport coaching, and sustainability and environmental studies. – *AB*

237

Trident Tech is state's largest two-year college

Trident Technical College is the largest public two-year college in South Carolina with 8,301 full-time equivalency students as of the fall of 2017. The multi-disciplinary college got its start in 1964 in North Charleston with the opening of the $1.7 million Berkeley-Charleston-Dorchester Technical Education Center, one of several regional facilities that were the brainchild of Gov. Ernest F. Hollings in 1961. On July 1, 1973, B-C-D Tech merged with Palmer College, a private business college on the Charleston peninsula, to become Trident Technical College.– *AB*

238

Public magnet arts school features a competitive audition for admission

Charleston County School of the Arts (SOA) in North Charleston, part of the Charleston County School District, is unlike any other school in the area. Founded in 1995 by Rose Maree Jordan Myers, who also served as the school's first principal until 2007, SOA serves more than 1,100 students in grades 6 through 12, but each of those students had to go through a rigorous admission process. Admission to SOA is based on a competitive audition in one of nine majors: creative writing, dance, instrumental band, piano, string orchestra, theater arts, visual arts, vocal music and fashion and costume design. With such an exclusive student body, it's no wonder SOA is regarded as one of the best public schools in the state and nation. – *SB*

239

First medical institution—then and now

The Medical University of South Carolina, founded in 1824, was the first medical institution in the Southeast. In 2019, it was ranked the number one hospital in South Carolina by *U.S. News & World Report*. – *AB*

240

Best high school in America

Academic Magnet High School in North Charleston was ranked number 1 of all American high schools in 2019, according to *U.S. News & World Report*. According to the magazine, "Almost all courses offered at Academic Magnet High School are either honors or Advanced Placement courses, and every student completes an independent research project over their junior and senior years. Students' work has been published in multiple academic and professional journals. Students can stay connected with Wi-Fi access in the cafeteria and three computer labs." – *AB*

241

Band of Gold treasured by Citadel graduates

There's a giant statue of the "Band of Gold," a term for the Citadel ring treasured by graduates, at Johnson Hagood Stadium. Graduates often take selfies with the statue after the number of the current graduating class is changed by a locksmith. That happens annually after seniors receive their rings in a special ceremony. – *AB*

242

Charleston's MUSC is a regional hospital

The Medical University of South Carolina's main campus is located on more than 50 acres in downtown Charleston. Since its founding in 1824, it has grown into a regional health care powerhouse that operates eight hospitals in the state with 1,600 beds as well as more than 100 outreach sites, the MUSC College of Medicine and nearly 275 telehealth locations.– *AB*

243

Bulldogs serve as Citadel mascots for 100 years

The Citadel's iconic mascot, a fiery bulldog, has been represented in real life for about 100 years, with more than 20 in-the-flesh mascots serving the college. They've had great names, such as Mike, Duke, Joker and Colonel Ruff. And there have been 10 different mascots named Boo. – *AB*

244

MUSC is leading academic center

The Medical University of South Carolina is a leading health science academic and research center in Charleston. Its 800-bed referral and teaching hospital is buttressed by six colleges with more than 1,700 faculty members who educate and train about 3,000 students and 700 residents every year. – *AB*

245

College of Charleston has really old bricks

The oldest bricks on the campus of the College of Charleston are found at its Towell Library. Its foundation was part of barracks used during the Revolutionary War. – *AB*

246

Citadel receives top academic marks

U.S. *News & World Report* in 2019 ranked The Citadel first in two categories: #1 Best School for veterans in the South (second top-ranking in a row), and #1 Top Public School in the South offering up to a master's degree (ninth consecutive top ranking). – *AB*

247

Top children's trauma center located in Charleston

MUSC's Children's Health in Charleston is the only children's trauma center in South Carolina to receive Level 1 verification – the highest possible level – from the American College of Surgeons. – *AB*

248

A perk of higher-ranking Citadel students

Cadet officers with the highest rank earn the right to live in double-sized rooms in the iconic Padget-Thomas Barracks clock tower. – *AB*

249

Half of Charleston residents have college degrees

Just over half of Charleston residents over 25 years old – 51.4 percent – had bachelor's degrees or higher, according to the 2010? Census. As a comparison, almost 42 percent of Charleston County residents have a similar education, while just over one in four residents across the state have a four-year degree or better. – *AB*

250

Boys and girls educated side by side after nearly a century of separation.

The merger of three historic boys schools in 1964 – Porter Military Academy (founded in 1867), the Gaud School for Boys (founded in 1908) and the Watt School (founded in 1931) – led to the creation of the Episcopal-affiliated Porter-Gaud. The year following its first class of 1965, Porter-Gaud became one of the first schools in the South to adopt an open admissions policy, allowing all qualifying students to apply and enter the program. In 1972, it became coeducational, allowing women into the first three grades that year. By the fall of 1976, the program allowed girls at all levels into the school. – *SB*

251

All-girls school still educating girls today

Mary Vardrine McBee bought the property at 172 Rutledge Ave. to establish an independent college prep school for girls in the spring of 1909, dubbing it Ashley Hall. The school grew over time, and in 1948, the Ashley Hall Foundation was founded. The group purchased the school from McBee the next year. Since its founding, Ashley Hall has seen an incredible number of students walk through its corridors, including notable names like Former First Lady Barbara Bush. – *SB*

CP

THE PEOPLE OF THIS STRANGE LAND WORSHIP THEIR ANCESTORS, EAT LOTS OF RICE AND THEY TALK FUNNY...
WE'VE DISCOVERED CHINA?
NO, SAILOR – WE'VE DISCOVERED CHARLESTON.
ARIAIL©2020

People

252

Conroy's lush novels captured the essence of the Lowcountry

One of the Lowcountry's best-known authors, Pat Conroy spent his college years at The Citadel in Charleston. Conroy's debut novel, *The Boo* (1970) featured his alma mater. His books drip with beautiful descriptions of the Lowcountry and blend broad themes of family, the military and the post-World War II South. Conroy's most well-known books include *The Water is Wide* (1972), *The Great Santini* (1976), *The Lords of Discipline* (1980) and *The Prince of Tides* (1986). His book *South of Broad* (2009) was set in Charleston and covers the tales from Leopold Bloom King through the 1960s and 1980s. The book includes Charleston's darker legacy of racism and class divisions. He died March 4, 2016, at the age of 70. – *LS*

253

Riley ushers in second revival of Charleston

Joseph P. Riley Jr. has the distinction of being Charleston's longest-serving mayor with many successes, including the founding of the International African American Museum. Riley, born in Charleston in 1943, attended The Citadel in Charleston and then the University of South Carolina in Columbia. First elected to the S.C. House of Representatives in 1968, he served three terms as a legislator, quickly earning a reputation as a reformer. Riley was elected mayor of Charleston in 1975. During his 10 terms in office, Charleston experienced a cultural renaissance through the initiation of several arts festivals, including Spoleto Festival USA, Piccolo Spoleto and the MOJA African American Arts Festival. Charleston became a top tourism destination thanks to the festivals and the economic revitalization of the city's historic district. Riley retired as mayor in 2016. – *LS*

254

Comedian Bill Murray makes Charleston his home

Funnyman and widely-known actor Bill Murray, who makes Charleston his home, is part-owner and "director of fun" of the Charleston RiverDogs, the city's South Atlantic League minor league baseball team. He's often at the park during the regular season, periodically rollicking with fans and players. The team's majority owner is New Jersey businessman Marv Goldklang of the Goldklang Group. Minority owners include locals Gene Budig and Al Phillips, as well as Peter Freund of Pound Ridge, New York. The team's president and general manager is Dave Echols, who has been with the franchise since 2004. – *AB*

255

Native Rucker is global ambassador for city's beauty

Darius Rucker, longtime frontman for Hootie & the Blowfish, was born in Charleston in 1966 and still lives in the area. He started the band in 1986 with three fellow rockers while they were students at the University of South Carolina. Rucker, whose distinctive rich voice mesmerizes audiences, and the band recorded six studio albums, including the smash 1994 debut, *Cracked Rear View.* In 2008, Rucker launched a solo career as a country music artist and continues to rack up awards, such as being named Country Music Association's new artist of the year in 2009. By 2019, he had recorded five solo country albums. – *AB*

256

Fantasy author James Rigney's life before writing

James Oliver Rigney Jr. (1948-2007), son of a Charleston Naval Shipyard supervisor, taught himself to read early and developed a lifelong reading habit. His library held more than 14,000 books when he died. After he played football at Clemson University for a season, he left the college to enlist in the U.S. Army. He served two tours in Vietnam, spending part of that time as a helicopter door gunner. He later earned a degree from The Citadel in physics and joined the Navy as a nuclear engineer. In 1977, after an accidental fall on a submarine shattered his knee and leg, Rigney spent part of his lengthy recovery writing his first fantasy novel, the still-unpublished *Warriors of the Altaii.* A Charleston bookshop owner introduced him to the poet and editor Harriet McDougal, whom he dated and eventually married. Rigney wrote seven Conan the Barbarian novels from 1982 to 1984 under the pseudonym Robert Jordan. – *City Paper (Paul Bowers)*

257

Rigney's series compared to Tolkien's work

In 1990, Rigney began writing his masterwork under the name Robert Jordan. It became the 14-volume Wheel of Time series, which critics compared favorably to the work of J.R.R. Tolkien for its sprawling story arcs and its complex integration of mythology and history. At the time of his death in 2007, he had sold more than 30 million books. But the Wheel of Time series wasn't finished. Rigney left behind a detailed outline for the end of the series, and his wife and editor chose the writer Brandon Sanderson to pen the final three volumes. (By the way, the College of Charleston's Addlestone Library is now the home of the James Rigney Collection, which includes first editions, video interviews and an Apple computer containing 4,000 pages worth of Rigney's notes that he used to write the series.) – *City Paper (Paul Bowers)*

258

Clementa Pinckney proved his civic, religious leadership

Clementa C. Pinckney (1973-2015) served as a state senator and senior pastor of the historically significant Emanuel African Methodist Episcopal Church in Charleston before he and eight worshippers were gunned down June 17, 2015, by a white nationalist from South Carolina. The murders during a Wednesday prayer service stunned the nation. President Barack Obama delivered a eulogy to 6,000 mourners at Pinckney's funeral on June 26, memorably closing his 40-minute address by singing the first verse of "Amazing Grace." Pinckney, elected to represent a rural district in the S.C. House in 1997, won a Senate race in 2000 to represent parts of five counties. Widely seen as a gentle giant of a leader, he didn't speak often, but when he did, his rich baritone voice resonated with calm and conviction. – *AB*

259

Jonathan Green paints with vibrancy

Painter and printmaker Jonathan Green, born in 1955 in rural Gardens Corner in Beaufort County, is known for bold use of vibrant colors in iconic Lowcountry scenes reflecting African American traditions. His popular work, seen throughout Charleston in offices, homes, museums and retail shops, is filled with references to "memories of local African American traditions, as well as tales and stories told by members of his extended family and friends," according to museum curator Jay Williams. "The artist's paintings reflect an authentic historical understanding of Lowcountry culture, although he sometimes takes poetic license with his subject matter. Green's Lowcountry subjects may or may not be factually realistic, but they communicate a strong sense of conceptual accuracy." Green lives in the Charleston area today. – *AB*

260

Ernest F. "Fritz" Hollings put performance over promise

U.S. Sen. and Gov. Ernest F. "Fritz" Hollings (1922-2019), a Charleston native with a larger-than-life charm and intelligence dedicated to using public policy to help South Carolinians, gave seven decades of public service – from serving as a young officer in World War II to becoming governor to being elected seven times to the United States Senate. His record of policy achievements was unmatched in modern times. As a young state representative in the 1950s, he pushed through stable funding for public schools. As governor, he established the state's banner technical education system, which attracted hundreds of companies. As senator, he led major policy initiatives to protect oceans, thwart hunger, promote a telecommunications revolution and save taxpayer money. His humor was legendary with talk peppered with aphorisms such as, "That's like the fireplug wetting the dog," or "There's no education in the second kick of a mule." The longest-serving junior senator in history, he retired in 2005 but continued to raise millions of dollars for cancer research. – *AB*

261

First to ask for federal building to be renamed

In what is considered an enormous example of humility, the late U.S. Sen. Fritz Hollings asked members of Congress to remove his name from a federal building and replace it with the name of Waties Waring, the courageous South Carolina federal judge who masterminded the nation's shift from segregated schools in a key 1951 opinion. U.S. Rep. Jim Clyburn, one of the nation's most powerful congressmen, said in 2015 that Hollings's request was the first in American history of someone asking his name to be removed from a federal building to honor someone else. Hollings, who was honored by the original naming of a federal courthouse annex in his honor in the 1980s, always thought the building should be named for Waring because of his courage to challenge the "separate but equal" standard in public education. "The request ... speaks volumes about his character and leadership," U.S. Sen. Lindsey Graham, R-S.C., observed. – *AB*

262

Scott is nation's only Black Republican U.S. senator

North Charleston native Tim Scott is the nation's only Black Republican member of the United States Senate. A graduate of R.B. Stall High School and Charleston Southern University, Scott owned an insurance agency and worked as a financial adviser before entering Congress. First elected to Charleston County Council in 1995, he became chair in 2007. The next year, he ran for a seat in the S.C. House, becoming the first Black Republican to win a seat in the chamber in more than 100 years. In 2010, Scott won a seat in the U.S. House. On Jan. 3, 2013, he was sworn in as a member of the Senate after being appointed by then-Gov. Nikki Haley to fill a seat vacated by U.S. Sen. Jim DeMint. Scott won an election in 2014 to finish DeMint's term, followed by a 2016 victory for a full six-year term. – *AB*

263

Locally-born Furchgott won Nobel Prize

American pharmacologist and Nobel Prize-winner Robert F. Furchgott was born June 4, 1916, in Charleston. He credited his upbringing in the Lowcountry marshes for his early interest in natural history and science. Along with Louis J. Ignarro and Ferid Murad, Furchgott won the Nobel Prize in Physiology or Medicine in 1998 for the discovery that nitric oxide acts as a signaling molecule in the cardiovascular system, making it a new mechanism by which blood vessels in the body widen. Their research led to nitric oxide being used to help overcome impotence with the drug Viagra. Researchers also suggested nitric oxide could be a key to improved treatments for heart disease, shock and cancer. Most of his work was while he was at State University of New York Downstate Health Sciences University, a public medical school and hospital in New York City. – *LS*

264

Shepard Fairey forever changes presidential posters

Charleston native and street artist Shepard Fairey is best known for his iconic "Hope" poster that supported Barack Obama's 2008 presidential campaign. But Fairey's graphic art has long been familiar on Charleston streets, windows and telephone boxes through his "Obey Giant" sticker campaign. He developed the homage to wrestler and actor Andre the Giant that reportedly was originally developed in 1989 while he attended the Rhode Island School of Design. According to ObeyGiant.com, "The OBEY sticker campaign can be explained as an experiment in Phenomenology. ... Phenomenology attempts to enable people to see clearly something that is right before their eyes but obscured; things that are so taken for granted that they are muted by abstract observation." Fairey's bold imagery is in collections around the country. He and his family live in Los Angeles. His parents live in Charleston. – *AB*

265

Popular writer Siddons adopted Charleston as home

Anne Rivers Siddons was born Sybil Anne Rivers on Jan. 9, 1936, in Fairburn, Georgia. Her novel-writing career began in 1976 with *Heartbreak Hotel.* Her novel *The House Next Door* (1978) was called one of the best horror novels of the 20th century by Stephen King. Siddons published 19 novels and one collection of essays. She moved to Charleston in 1998 where she wrote *Low Country* (1998), *Nora, Nora* (2000), *Islands* (2004) and *Sweetwater Creek* (2005). Siddons died Sept. 11, 2019. – *LS*

266

Outdoorsman Ben Moise spins great yarns

Outdoorsman Ben Moise (1943-) grew up near Sumter, but has spent much of his adult life in Charleston. He wrote the best-selling book *Ramblings of a Lowcountry Game Warden,* published in 2008. The book was based on his work as a conservation officer with the S.C. Department of Natural Resources from 1978 to 2002. In recognition of his career in law enforcement, Moise earned the Guy Bradley Award by the North American Fish and Wildlife Foundation in 1990. He received the Order of the Palmetto from S.C. Gov. Carroll Campbell in 1994. Moise remains a contributor to *The (Charleston) Post and Courier,* the *Charleston Mercury,* the *Charleston City Paper* and other regional publications. – *LS*

267

Pinckney played key role in literary revival

Writer Josephine Pinckney, born Jan. 25, 1895, played a key role in the literary revival that swept through the South after World War I. She worked closely with DuBose Heyward, Hervey Allen and John Bennett in founding the Poetry Society of South Carolina in 1920. Pinckney gained a national reputation for her poetry, often eulogies to a vanishing way of Southern life. Her only book of poems was *Sea-Drinking Cities* (1927). Pinckney also helped with the transcriptions and musical annotations for the African-American songs included in *The Carolina Lowcountry* (1931). In 1941, Pinckney published her first novel, *Hilton Head,* followed by the best-selling social comedy *Three O'Clock Dinner* (1945), which made her one of America's best-known women fiction writers. She wrote three more novels before her death Oct. 4, 1957. – *LS*

268

Halsey earned a long list of achievements for his artwork

Artist William Halsey, born March 13,1915 in Charleston, had talent that shone through from a young age. Encouraged by his mother, he completed studies at the Museum School of Fine Arts in Boston and a two-year fellowship in Mexico before returning to Charleston. He then befriended Merton Simpson, a young African-American artist. Halsey provided the teenager with private instruction as segregation disallowed Simpson from attending the Gibbes Museum where Halsey was the director of art classes. The two maintained a lifelong friendship as Halsey went on to teach at the College of Charleston, have an art gallery at the Simons Fine Arts Center (now the Halsey Institute) and earn an honorary degree from the College of Charleston in 1995. After his death in 1999, he posthumously received the Elizabeth O'Neill Verner Governor's Award for the arts for Lifetime Achievement, the state's highest award in the arts. – *SB*

269

One of the oldest YouTube sensations made his home in Charleston

Charles Marvin Green Jr., better known as Angry Grandpa, was an American internet personality before his death in December 2017 due to cirrhosis of the liver. The West Ashley resident's Youtube channel, "The Angry Grandpa Show," was just shy of 4.5 million subscribers in 2020, and his videos have been featured on *Dr. Drew,* TruTV's *Most Shocking, Rude Tube* and MTV's *Pranked.* The channel is still being updated, and more previously-filmed but unreleased videos of AGP were still being uploaded as recently as May 2, 2020. The content was filmed previously and had yet to be released. – *SB*

270

Maverick's most lasting legacy was perhaps the use of his name

Samuel Augustus Maverick, lawyer and land speculator, settled in San Antonio, Texas, after a Lowcountry upbringing. Bored with plantation life and unsuited to overseeing slaves, he sought cheap land westward and arrived in 1834 at the height of the Texas revolution. It was near the Gulf of Mexico that his legacy was cemented in history as he refused to brand the cattle he kept on the Matagorda Peninsula along the Gulf of Mexico. Legend has it that he believed this refusal gave him claim to all unbranded calves on the land, but in reality, he simply never bothered to brand his small herd and wasn't in business long enough for it to matter. Still, the word "maverick" is still used as a term for unbranded cattle and to describe a person of highly unorthodox mindset, a memento of Maverick's time as a rancher and his strange ways. – *SB*

271

Morse painted portraits in Charleston

Before Samuel Morse created the internationally renowned Morse Code, he was one of Charleston's most fashionable portraitists. Morse was 26 when he arrived in the fall of 1817, coming with well-placed letters of introduction from individuals such as his father, Congressionalist minister Jebediah Morse, who was a friend of patriot Charles Cotesworth Pinckney. By the end of his first year in the state, Morse was getting $80 for each portrait, banking $3,500 worth in commissions – near $60,000 today. It wasn't until news of the 1825 death of his wife, who was buried before he could reach home due to a delay in the news, that he dedicated himself to finding a quicker way to communicate across long distances, thus birthing Morse Code. – *SB*

272

Colbert revealed favorite Charleston stomping grounds

Long before comedian Stephen Colbert took over as host of television's *Late Show,* he was just like many other Charlestonians with a love of swimming, fishing and skating down the streets of what he remembers being a "sleepy Southern town." Today, Charleston is still one of his favorite vacation spots, and he isn't shy about sharing some of his go-to places. To stay: The Francis Marion Hotel and the Mills House Wyndham Grand Hotel. To eat: Hominy Grill (now closed) and Husk. And to shop: what he calls the district with "no chains," King Street. – *SB*

273

Golfer Daniel's symmetrical hall of fame induction

Charleston native Beth Daniel met the Ladies Professional Golf Association's Hall of Fame entrance requirements in February 1999. But she postponed her official induction until 2000, the 50th anniversary of the LPGA Tour – and the year her parents celebrated their 50th wedding anniversary. Daniel was a *tour de force* as a pro golfer with 46 victories under her belt, including the 1990 LPGA Championship, 32 additional LPGA Tour wins and five Solheim Cup wins. She is also a three-time LPGA Player of the Year, taking the title in 1980, 1990 and 1994. – *SB*

274

Frank returns home for book-writing venture

Dorothea "Dot" Benton Frank was born Sept. 12, 1951, on Sullivan's Island. Her debut novel *Sullivan's Island: A Lowcountry Tale* (1999) was published after she decided to write a book to earn enough money to buy back her mother's house on Sullivan's Island. It sold more than 1 million copies, but the house had already sold, so she purchased another home on the island outside Charleston. She went on to write 19 more best-selling novels that usually featured strong, complex women and family conflicts. Her last book, *Queen Bee* (2019), eschewed the cheating husbands and terrible in-laws common to her novels to focus on a beekeeping, single teacher living on Sullivan's Island. She lived in Montclair, N.J., and Sullivan's Island until her death in 2019. – *LS*

275

Kidd explores Charleston in 2014 novel

Author Sue Monk Kidd, born in 1948 in Albany, Georgia, was raised 25 miles away in Sylvester, where she said stories told to her by her father and the Black women who worked in the family home influenced her later writings. She moved to South Carolina in the 1970s. Kidd published her debut novel, *The Secret Life of Bees,* in 2002. The novel spent more than two years on *The New York Times* bestseller list. Kidd's two subsequent novels, *The Mermaid Chair* (2005) and *The Invention of Wings* (2014), are both set in South Carolina, with the latter in Charleston. She currently lives in North Carolina. – *LS*

276

Greene's books showcase Charleston's Jewish and gay cultures

Harlan Greene is a fiction and nonfiction writer whose work often centers on Charleston, homosexuality and Jewish identity. Greene, born in 1953 in Charleston to Holocaust survivors. has worked at the South Carolina Historical Society, Charleston County Public Library, and the Avery Research Center for African American History and Culture in Charleston. In 2020, he was the senior manuscript and reference archivist at the College of Charleston's Addlestone Library. Greene's debut novel, *Why We Never Danced the Charleston* (1984), examines Charleston's gay culture in the 1920s. *What the Dead Remember* (1991) is a coming-of-age story set in Charleston. It won the Lambda Literary Award for Gay Fiction. Greene has also penned several nonfiction works related to Charleston. – *LS*

277

White pens mystery series inspired by Tradd Street

Born May 30, 1964, in Tulsa, Okla., Karen White grew up in London and now lives with her husband near Atlanta. She is known for her Tradd Street mystery series, which is based in Charleston. This first book in the series, *The House on Tradd Street*, was published in 2008. There are six books in the series, the most recent being *The Christmas Spirits on Tradd Street*, published in 2019. – *LS*

278

Lott writes, teaches in Charleston area

A novelist, short story writer, memoirist and educator, Bret Lott was born Oct. 8, 1948, in Los Angeles, Calif. He came to South Carolina in 2004 as a writer-in-residence and professor at the College of Charleston, where he still teaches. Most of his works were published in the 1980s and 1990s, including *A Stranger's House, Jewel, Reed's Beach,* and two short story collections. Known for his family-driven narratives, Lott diverted in two more recent mystery books with the character Huger Dillard in *The Hunt Club* (1998) and *Dead Low Tide* (2012). Lott and his family live in Hanahan, a city outside of Charleston. – *LS*

279

Simms's 19th century poetry conveys beauty, mystery of state

Born in Charleston April 17, 1806, William Gilmore Simms was raised by his grandmother who told tales of Charleston during the Revolutionary War. He lacked a formal education but became an avid traveler and reader. In 1829, Simms became editor of the *City Gazette,* a Charleston newspaper through which he railed against nullification and John C. Calhoun's doctrine that states could block federal law. In 1833, he embarked on his literary career with his first work of fiction, a ghost story, *Martin Faber.* He went on to write a series of Georgia frontier border tales, *The Yemassee* (1835), and Revolutionary War romances. Scholars say Simms's principal contributions to a broader understanding of South Carolina are through his poetry, history, biographies and fiction. Simms's best poetry, such as "Maid of Congaree" and "Dark-Eyed Maid of Edisto," conveyed the beauty and mystery of South Carolina. He died in Charleston in 1870. His bust is at White Point Garden. – *LS*

280

Peterkin becomes first S.C. author to win Pulitzer

Author Julia Peterkin was born on Halloween in 1880 in Laurens County. She later lived in Spartanburg and near St. Matthew. Although there are no accounts of her living in Charleston, Peterkin is seen as a key player in the Charleston Renaissance, a cultural revival that took place in the years between World Wars I and II. She did not begin her writing career until she was 40 years old. But her debut novel *Scarlet Sister Mary* (1928) was set in the Lowcountry, and featured Black characters and their struggles in Jim Crow South, then an unusual subject for a white Southern writer. It earned her early scorn and the banning of the book from at least one public library in South Carolina. But it also earned her a Pulitzer, making her the first honoree from South Carolina. Today, Peterkin is recognized for serious depictions of the African American experience and rank descriptions of sex. She died Aug. 10, 1961, in Orangeburg. – *LS*

281

Monroe captivated by Lowcountry's beauty. fragility

Mary Alice Monroe, a *New York Times* bestselling author of 23 novels, is a South Carolina resident known for fiction that explores compelling parallels between nature and humanity. A frequent speaker at book festivals, conferences and private events, Monroe immersed herself in academic research and hands-on volunteering to learn about conservation issues. She uses that knowledge and experience to craft captivating stories with powerful man-versus-nature themes. She has worked with bottlenose dolphins, monarch butterflies, shorebirds and loggerhead sea turtles, each of which have been worked into her novels. Beyond provocative novels, Monroe has also published two children's books which complement the environmental themes she's known for. – *SB*

282

Wentworth serves as South Carolina's poet laureate

Born June 3, 1958, in Lynn, Massachusetts, Marjory Heath Wentworth moved to the Charleston area when she and her family settled on Sullivan's Island. In the next decade, Wentworth began teaching creative writing in the region and state. Her books of poetry include *Noticing Eden* (2003), *Despite Gravity* (2007), and *The Endless Repetition of an Ordinary Miracle* (2012). Her children's story, *Shackles* (2009), is set in Sullivan's Island and explores the island's history of wealthy white people enslaving other people. Wentworth read her poem "Rivers of Wind" at the inauguration of Gov. Mark Sanford in January 2003. That same year, she was named the state's poet laureate, a title she continued to hold in 2020. In 2016 with journalist Herb Frazier and historian Bernard Powers, she co-authored *We Are Charleston*, a touching reflection on the tragedy and triumph of a 2015 shooting that killed nine worshippers at Emanuel AME Church and galvanized a nation.. – *LS*

283

Humphreys inspired by Lowcountry landscape after a rocky graduation

Novelist Josephine Humphreys, born in 1945 in Charleston, was encouraged by her grandmother Neta, and later by her mother, to write. She attended Duke University, which her dad thought was a "southern university" because he was against her going to any "northern school." Much to his surprise, however, Humphreys was in the school's first racially-integrated undergraduate class, which didn't seem to be an issue until a bomb threat from the Ku Klux Klan on graduation day. Humphreys has said a lot of her work, such as *Rich in Love* and *The Fireman's Fair*, have been inspired by the landscape of Charleston as well as her own life. Most importantly, though, they reflect Charleston and how it has changed between her childhood and today. In recent years, Humphreys was a founder of the private Facebook group, Charleston History before 1945, which had more than 35,000 members in 2020. – *SB*

284

Gilbreth was popular post World War II columnist, author

Frank Bunker Gilbreth Jr., born March 17, 1911, in Plainfield New Jersey, lived an ordinary life in New Jersey until World War II, during which he served as a naval officer in the South Pacific. He participated in three invasions in the Admiralty Islands and the Philippines. He was decorated with two air medals and a bronze star. After the war, in 1947, he relocated to Charleston, and found his place at *The Post and Courier,* the city's main daily newspaper, as an editorial writer and columnist. But, he got national attention for writing the bestseller *Cheaper by the Dozen* in 1948 and its sequel, *Belles on Their Toes,* in 1950 with his older sister, Ernestine. At the newspaper, Gilbreth used the pen name Ashley Cooper for a long-running column, *Doing the Charleston,* which featured good gossip, jokes and community commentary. Gilbreth retired from the paper as assistant publisher and vice president in 2001. He died in February 2001. – *SB*

285

Patton is a highly-decorated actor, audiobook narrator

Actor and native Charlestonian Will Patton, born June 14, 1954, has won two Obie Awards for best actor for his roles in Sam Shepard's play *Fool for Love* and the public theater production of *What Did He See?.* He is the son of playwright and acting/directing instructor Bill Patton, who also later served as a chaplain at Duke University. Along with his long list of on-screen appearances in movies like *Remember the Titans* and *Armageddon,* the younger Patton also boasts almost as long of a list of voice work in audiobooks written by greats Stephen King, Charles Bukowski, James Lee Burke and more. – *SB*

286

Gibson goes from Little Theater to big screen

Thomas E. Gibson, a well-known television and film actor born in Charleston in 1962, attended Little Theater School and belonged to the Young Charleston Theater Company and Footlight Players. He attended the College of Charleston before winning a Juilliard School Drama Division scholarship. He has appeared in many movies including *Eyes Wide Shut* (1999) and *Son of Batman* (2014). He played Greg in the popular ABC show *Dharma & Greg,* which ran from 1997 until 2002, and was nominated for two Golden Globes for that role. In 2016, after four seasons with the CBS drama *Criminal Minds,* Gibson was fired in the wake of an on-set altercation with a producer. He continues to act and currently resides in Texas. – *LS*

287

Pollitzer sisters are trailblazers for women's rights

Three Charleston sisters – Carrie, Mabel and Anita Pollitzer – were famous suffragists and women's rights campaigners recognized across the state and nationally for their work. They were daughters of Gustave M. Pollitzer, a cotton broker, and Clara Guinzburg, daughter of a rabbi from Austria. In 1900, the family moved to a home at 5 Pitt Street in Charleston just blocks from the College of Charleston campus. In addition to their civic work and community involvement, the sisters also took active roles in the congregation of Kahal Kadosh Beth Elohim, the first Reform Judaism congregation in the United States. – *AB*

288

The petitioning sister

Carrie Teller Pollitzer (1881-1974) was a charter member of the Charleston Equal Suffrage League and launched the petition drive that led to the admission of women to the College of Charleston in 1918. When told $1,200 was needed to effect coeducation, she organized a mass meeting at the Chamber of Commerce and raised more than $1,500. Carrie Pollitzer "studied at, and later directed, the South Carolina Kindergarten Training School in Charleston, where she established public health programs, home visits, kindergarten lunches, and parental-involvement programs," according to *The South Carolina Encyclopedia.* – *LS*

289

The teaching sister

Mabel Louise Pollitzer (1885-1979), obtained legislation establishing the Charleston County Free Library in 1929. A biology teacher for 44 years at Memminger High School, she organized an early school lunch program there. "To encourage student interest in gardens, she organized a 'Plant Exchange Day' in March 1915. The Civic Club helped sponsor what became an annual citywide event," The South Carolina Encyclopedia said. Mabel Pollitzer also was chair and publicity director of the state National Woman's party. She was a vocal supporter for suffrage and then for the Equal Rights Amendment, which she campaigned for until her death. - *LS*

290

The art sister

Anita Lily Pollitzer (1894-1975) is credited with showing the drawings of an unknown artist, Georgia O'Keeffe, to photographer Alfred Steglitz, which launched the artist's career. For Anita Pollitzer, Steglitz served as a "mentor in modernism" while she studied at Columbia University, from which she received a bachelor's degree in fine arts in 1916 and a master's degree in international relations in 1933. Liker her sisters, Anita Pollitzer spent years fighting for women's rights. Her biography of O'Keeffe, *A Woman on Paper*, was published posthumously in 1988, as was her selected correspondence with the artist in 1990. – *LS*

291

Move to Charleston sparked *American Idol* top-sixer's music career

Singer Elise Testone moved to Charleston in 2006, only a year after graduating from Coastal Carolina University in Conway with a bachelor's degree in music. Shortly after the move, she began collaborating with local rock, pop, funk and soul musicians while writing her own blues and jazz pieces. In July 2011, she auditioned for American Idol in North Charleston, where she received numerous standing ovations for her performances as she climbed her way to the top six. In October 2011, Testone and her band, The Freeloaders, won the Funk/Soul/R&B Artist of the Year award in the *Charleston City Paper's* Music issue, and additional recognition from the *CP* later in the year, winning the staff pick for Best Tribute for Elise Testone's James Brown Dance Party. – *SB*

292

War hero Clark served as president of The Citadel

Army Gen. Mark Clark, who served in both world wars as a high-ranking officer, was considered a brilliant "trainer of men" by future President Dwight D. Eisenhower. Clark earned 27 medals and awards during his service, including the Distinguished Service Cross for the World War II battle at Salerno. After his military retirement in 1953, he served as the president of The Citadel in Charleston until 1956, during which time he also headed the "Clark Task Force," which studied and made recommendations on all intelligence activities of the federal government. Clark, who died on April 17, 1984, just before his 88th birthday, was the last surviving four-star officer from World War II. He is buried on the Citadel campus. Some also remember him for a rocky military campaign in Italy from 1943 to 1945, which included an unsuccessful assault on the Gari River in 1944.

293

Charleston native finds big success on Wall Street

Sallie L. Krawcheck described her childhood in Charleston as "half-Jewish, half WASP-y," an upbringing she credits for her later successes as a top Wall Street analyst and executive. In 2002, *Fortune* magazine dubbed her "the last honest analyst." About that time, she became CEO of Smith Barney for Citigroup, later being appointed as its chief financial officer. In 2007, she took over as CEO of Citi's wealth management business, which included Smith Barney. Through the years, she was on the covers of top business magazines and major lists, such as being named in 2008 to *Investment Advisor* magazine's IA 25, the list of the 25 most influential people in and around the investment advisory business. After a 2009 move to Bank of America to head its Merrill Lynch division and numerous other accolades, she kickstarted her own digital financial advisor platform geared for women in 2016 by starting Ellevest. She also owned and chaired the Ellevate Network in 2020.

294

Witte may be best example of the poetry group's influence

Beatrice Witte Ravenel, born in Charleston in August 1870, entered the Harvard Annex (later Radcliffe College) as a special student in 1889, studying for a few years before leaving and finally returning in 1895 for two more years. The founding of the Poetry Society of South Carolina in 1920, the year of Ravenel's husband's death, brought her into a poetry-conscious environment, prompting great changes in her work. Ravenel's poetry in the 1920s explored outsiders and the dispossessed, such as the Yemassee Indians, and a young actress, soon to die, musing on her young son. After a book of her poems, edited by fellow Charlestonian Louis Rubin, was published in 1969, scholars and critics began to hail her as the best poet of the Charleston Renaissance. She died on March 15, 1956, but was posthumously inducted into the South Carolina Academy of Authors in 1995. – *SB*

CP

Lowcountry attractions

295

Two Civil War forts are now national monuments operated by the National Park Service

Visitors to the Lowcountry and natives can now experience the rich history of Forts Sumter and Moultrie up close and personal. The National Park Service's (NPS) Fort Sumter Tour begins at Liberty Square and the NPS visitor center; guests take a boat out to the small island in Charleston Harbor, and follow in the footsteps of Civil War soldiers who fought there. Fort Moultrie's grounds are a bit more easily accessed, resting on Sullivan's Island. – *SB*

296

Colonial-era home grants visitors a ticket to the past

The Nathaniel Russell House Museum offers a glimpse into the lives of the mercantile elite who found their success in the late colonial and early federal period of Charleston. The artisans and craftsmen these merchants commissioned to build and decorate their homes, and the enslaved men and women whose labor made their lifestyles possible are also honored and remembered within the walls of the historic home. The defining characteristic of the home is a three-story cantilevered flying staircase, whose "sweep is broad, treads are deep and the rise perfectly proportioned and easy of ascent," according to Nathaniel Russell's great-granddaughter, Alicia Hopton Middleton. – *SB*

297

Magnolia Plantation in same family for three centuries

Magnolia Plantation and Gardens has been owned by the same family since the late 1670s, according to the program director and historian, Caroline Howell. When Thomas Drayton and his wife, Ann, arrived from Barbados in 1676, they unknowingly became the first in a direct line of Magnolia family ownership that has lasted more than 300 years. – *SB*

298

Magnolia one of five in the U.S. to receive prestigious award

Magnolia Plantation and Gardens is one of only five gardens in the U.S. to be awarded the International Camellia Garden of Excellence award, a prestigious honor from the International Camellia Society. "I get to take America's oldest public garden into the future," said Director of Gardens Tom Johnson in a *Southern Living* article. "Magnolia is a lady, and my job is to shine her shoes and dress her in robes for the thousands of suitors who come courting." – *SB*

299

Magnolia recognized by Karl Baedeker following American Civil War

Only three places in the country received a two-star review from Karl Baedeker in 1893, whose company, Baedeker, set the standard for authoritative guidebooks for tourists. They were the Grand Canyon, Niagara Falls, and Magnolia Gardens.

This recognition came shortly after the Gardens were burned during the American Civil War, after which all but 390 acres of the plantation were sold by John Drayton to raise money in the wake of the war's economic devastation. – *SB*

300

Modern classic partly inspired by Magnolia's Audubon Swamp Garden

The Audubon Swamp Garden at Magnolia Plantation and Gardens was used for inspiration from the movie *Shrek* after its art director was chased by an alligator in the area. This fun fact was mentioned on Magnolia's Facebook page in 2016. The original post can still be found, a classic image of the green ogre's face and all, with a little digging. – *SB*

301

How many cans of Silly String did the Charleston RiverDogs use?

The Charleston RiverDogs, a popular minor-league baseball team with the motto "Fun Is Good," is a leader in sports entertainment across the Lowcountry. Its motto, developed by club President Emeritus and showman Mike Veeck, serves a guideline and reminder for how ballplayers and employees of the organization, which is affiliated with the New York Yankees, should approach their jobs and, in turn, capture the imagination of fans. The team is known for rollicking promotions, such as Go Back to Ohio Night, Nobody Night and Silent Night. In 2017, fans used 4,025 cans of Silly String during Silly String Night, later named one of the best promotions of the year. – *AB*

302

Largest known flying bird fossil on display

The Charleston Museum contains the fossil remains of the Pelagornis, the world's largest known flying bird that lived 26 million years ago. The fossil was found at the Charleston International Airport. The Pelagornis has the largest wingspan of any active flapping birds so far discovered. Although some pterosaurs and other extinct animals may have had larger wingspans than Pelagornis, these most likely relied solely on gliding. – *SB*

303

Archaeological digs unearth pieces of past and present

Fragments from a seagrass basket made by enslaved people in the 18th century were recovered during a series of archaeological projects at the Charleston Museum's Heyward-Washington House throughout the 1990s and early 2000s. Modern craftsmen said the old basket's weave is the same weave they use today. Bonus: The Heyward-Washington House was the first house museum opened in South Carolina. – *SB*

304

Original European settlement designated as a historical site

Charles Towne Landing is one of only a handful of original settlement sites that still exist in the United States. It was also the first permanent European settlement in South Carolina according to South Carolina State Parks, dating back to 1670. The site is now home to a replica of a 17th century trading vessel visitors can board and explore called *Adventure*. The ship was designed by renowned 20th century shipwright William Avery Baker in 1969. – *SB*

305

New museum dedicated to African-American heritage to open in 2022

The International African American Museum, a two-decade project on the Cooper River with views of Fort Sumter, is expected to open in 2022 on land that was the disembarkation point for up to 40 percent of enslaved Africans brought to America. There, at what was known as Gadsden's Wharf, they awaited their fate – sale into the plantation economy. The campaign to build the museum was led by former mayor Joseph P. Riley Jr., and involved some of the Lowcountry's most influential leaders, institutions and community members. They raised millions of dollars from corporate, government and private coffers to build a place to honor untold stories of the estimated 388,000 Africans shipped into North America. – *SB and AB*

306

Charleston's City Market rose from the ashes

The Charleston City Market, now a must-see for visitors and residents alike, has survived an incredible number of natural disasters, including two fires, the first of which, in 1796, led to the building's total reconstruction and rebranding of the city's Beef Market into a new "Centre Market." In turn, that market eventually was named the City Market that we know today. The second fire in 1838 destroyed the Centre Market's head-house, which was rebuilt and dubbed the Market Hall in 1841 based on a design by local architect Edward B. White. – *SB*

307

The many names given to the Charleston City Market's historical observer and janitor

The birds that historically frequented the Charleston City Market during the late 1700s and early 1800s, especially after dogs were banned from the premises in 1799, were nicknamed "Charleston buzzards" and "Charleston eagles." In reality, these birds were black vultures – scavenging birds of prey native to the Lowcountry which were attracted to the scraps of meat and fish from the market. (If the same person who renamed cockroaches as "Palmetto bugs" had been involved with these flesh-eaters, we bet they would have been genteely named "Palmetto birds!") – *SB*

308

Don't touch that bird!

Downtown Charleston's black vultures were assumed by foreign visitors and locals alike to have been protected by law, due to the services they provided as natural janitors. However, no such law existed. Some historians believe that there were rules and regulations posted by the Charleston City Market discouraging or prohibiting people from harming the vultures, and over time the signage was misconstrued as law. – *SB*

309

Charleston's three markets offered variety

Long before the Charleston City Market was established, and even before the Charleston Beef Market was consolidated on a newly-constructed Market Street, the city's markets were split into three. If you wanted to buy fresh beef, you would visit the beef market at Broad and Meeting streets. Small meats like lamb and pork were sold at the Lower Market at the end of Tradd Street. And fish, fruits, and vegetables were sold at the east end of Queen Street, well before Vendue Range and Waterfront Park were in place. – *SB*

310

The real story behind the misnomer of Charleston's City Market

Standing on the site of a filled-in creek and marshy land donated to the city in 1788, the Charleston City Market is no stranger to misnomers and misinformation. Known to many as the "Old Slave Market," the myth that slaves were once sold within its walls is perpetuated still today. In fact, no slaves were ever sold at this location, and some think the name is actually derived from its historical status as the market at which slaves and freemen would do their shopping. – *SB*

311

Ever wonder how Vendue Range got its name?

Later down the line, after the market stands for fish and vegetables at the eastern end of Queen Street closed in the late 1780s and early 1790s, a new type of market began to surface. Along the short road at the end of Queen Street, ranges of commercial buildings arose. While they weren't set up for retail sales, they were perfect for vendue sales. "Vendue" is an Old English word for sale at public outcry, or auction. And this spontaneous market – what we would call a popup sale today – is what gave name to the short road leading to Waterfront Park—Vendue Range. – *SB*

312

Charleston Music Hall's historic foundations

The Charleston Music Hall on John Street sat vacant and run-down for more than 60 years after the Bagging Manufacturing Company, which made woven fiber bags for cotton, closed in the aftermath of the Charleston earthquake in August, 1886. The earthquake had destroyed a three-story tower, and most of the building was demolished, with the rest being used for little more than storage. – *SB*

313

Skaggs wins Grammy for live album recorded in Charleston Music Hall

In 1995, the Bennett-Hofford Company pulled the derelict Charleston Music Hall out of the grave and transformed it into an arts venue. After its revitalization, renowned bluegrass musician Ricky Skaggs won a Grammy Award for his live album, *Ricky Skaggs and Kentucky Thunder: Live at the Charleston Music Hall.* The hall has also hosted performances by top music figures such as David Byrne and Joan Baez. – *SB*

314

American Classic Tea's Charlestonian roots

While the Charleston Tea Garden is not the country's first attempt at locally grown tea (that accolade goes to a small farm from colonial Georgia), it is the oldest tea plantation still in operation. It had a rocky start in Summerville in 1888, closing and reopening a number of times. But when the Thomas J. Lipton Company sold the property in 1987 to Mack Fleming and Bill Hal, they converted the farm into a functional tea garden. American Classic Tea was born. Currently, stores in 17 states stock the tea for commercial sale, primarily in the Eastern U.S. Check out Charleston Tea Garden's "Where to Buy" map for more information on how to get your hands on it. – *SB*

315

Southerners' equal love for sweet tea and America matched by plantation

According to the Charleston Tea Garden, its brand of tea is the only in the world made with 100 percent American-grown tea. The plantation is also strongly in touch with its Southern heritage and consumers, producing a tea custom-blended to be perfect for iced tea, in addition to a variety of other flavors and blends of green and black tea. – *SB*

316

Where to get married, get your mail, pay taxes, get divorced

The Four Corners of Law, a term coined by Robert Ripley in Ripley's Believe it or Not, is the intersection of Broad and Meeting streets in Charleston. It refers to the four buildings on each corner of the intersection: St. Michael's Church, built between 1752 and 1761; the Charleston County Courthouse, originally built in 1753 as South Carolina's provincial capital and later rebuilt in 1792 as a courthouse; Charleston City Hall, built between 1800 and 1804; and the United States Post Office and federal courthouse, built in 1896. Together, the four buildings represent four different institutions of law: religious, local, state and federal. – *SB*

317

Life from times past revived and preserved centuries later

Most of Middleton Place was burned just before the end of the Civil War. Then, just over two decades later, in 1886, the Great Earthquake shook it to its foundations and destroyed the walls of the main residence and north flanker building. Reconstruction began in 1925, and the historic landmark now features an award-winning modernized inn for guests that allows them to experience the lives of those who once called this place home. – *SB*

318

South Carolina Aquarium gets fishy in 2000

The South Carolina Aquarium, near the intersections of Calhoun and Concord streets, opened May 19, 2000. It was one of the many new parks and attractions to open under Mayor Joseph P. Riley, who helped to revitalize and grow the city over 10 terms from 1975 to 2016. The aquarium features a spectrum of species from the Southeast Appalachian watershed from the mountains to the coast. The nonprofit aquarium has received national recognition for its education initiatives on the state's regional aquatic ecosystems.– *LS*

319

Sea turtles' journey from rescue to recovery and release

The South Carolina Aquarium makes its home right on Downtown Charleston's coastal waters. With dozens of unique exhibits and attractions, it's difficult to narrow it down to one star, but it's even harder for anything to stand out against the Zucker Family Sea Turtle Recovery. "Both a hospital and a guest experience," reads the description, a reference to the fact that this exhibit makes the rehabilitation of injured and sick sea turtles visible to every visitor. – *SB*

320

Three relics of maritime history docked in Charleston Harbor

Patriot's Point, on the mouth of the Cooper River in Mt. Pleasant, is home to three large pieces of history, and is a previous home to a few others: the *USS Yorktown,* an aircraft carrier; the *USS Laffey,* a destroyer; and the *USS Clamagore,* a submarine to be sunk as an artificial reef. One of the notable previous ships docked in the harbor was the *NS Savannah,* America's first and only nuclear merchant vessel. It was kept at Patriot's Point until 1994. – *SB*

321

Expo brings awareness to conservation efforts for Lowcountry treasures

The Southeastern Wildlife Exposition, founded in 1982, has grown over time to become the largest event of its kind in the United States, attracting more than 500 artists and exhibitors from around the world and more than 40,000 attendees. A three-day celebration in February, SEWE has earned a reputation of excellence as it hosts some of the world's foremost wildlife experts and offers original artwork, diverse exhibits, school programs, informative presentations and fun events. Each year, SEWE aims to increase public awareness of Charleston's natural treasures and the need to protect and preserve them for the future. – *SB*

322

World-class 10k run held over Cooper River

The coronavirus pandemic of 2020 interrupted the annual Cooper River Bridge Run for the first time in its 43 years. Prior to 2020, up to 39,000 registered runners dashed from Mount Pleasant through Charleston's streets every spring. Started in 1978, the modern run spans across the Arthur Ravenel Jr. Bridge, 2.5 miles long and 200 feet above the water, granting incredible views to participants. The event raises funds for public education on the importance of exercise. – *SB*

CP

Miscellany: By the numbers

323

Not bad to be called SOB in Charleston

In Charleston, "SOB" stands for "South of Broad" Street and refers to the oldest part of the peninsular city. This area is residential today, featuring 18th- and 19th-century homes worth millions of dollars. Broad Street, once a boundary of the early 18th-century town, became a commercial hub of apothecaries, silversmiths and more before growing as a banking and legal center. Originally named Cooper Street, it was renamed in the middle of the 1700s to reflect a civic pride of the wide, commercial street flanked with the colony's Statehouse, churches and beautiful homes. – *AB*

324

Charleston has some funny-sounding street names

There are plenty of street names in Charleston that sound a whole lot different than they look. Why? Because of holdover European pronunciations mixed with Southern slurring and slang through the centuries. Some old French street names with Charleton linguistic twists: Beaufain (BU-fane), Huger (you-GEE), Legare (luh-GREE) and Prioleau (PRAY-lo) . Then there's Hassell (HAZE-ul) Street, the Gaillard (GILL-yard) Center and Vanderhorst Street, which can be pronounced VAN-dross or VAN-der-horst. There's a neighborhood called Mazyck (muh-ZEKE) Wraggsborough. And on Daniel Island, which technically is in the city of Charleston, there's a Lesesne (luh-SANE) Street. – *AB*

325

Highest point on the peninsula

The Indian Hill Water Tower on the campus of The Citadel is the highest point in the Charleston peninsula. It also is the former site of a Native American trader's home.– *AB*

326

Morris Island Lighthouse now surrounded by water

A navigation beacon first was built on Morris Island as early as 1673 to lead ships safely into Charleston harbor. Today's iconic white-and-red banded lighthouse is the third such structure to aid navigation. When originally built in its conical shape in 1876, it was located 1,200 feet from the sea. But decades of coastal erosion exacerbated by construction of jetties in Charleston harbor left the 161-foot tower offshore today. The lighthouse went out of service in 1962. Save the Light, a nonprofit, bought the lighthouse to preserve it and after a leasing deal with the state, it raised millions of dollars to build a steel cofferdam at its base to protect it. – *AB*

327

Citadel has lots of alumni and service hours

The Citadel has:

- More than 20,000 volunteer community service hours every year performed by cadets.
- 16 Division I athletic teams
- More than 39,000 alumni.– *AB*

328

Military school in *House of Cards* inspired by The Citadel

Francis Joseph Underwood, a fictional South Carolinian played by actor Kevin Spacey who is the lead protagonist of the American television adaptation of *House of Cards,* rose from being U.S. House majority whip to president of the United States through treachery, deception and murder. But before he could soar through fictionalized political ceilings, he graduated from the prestigious military college, The Sentinel. If that sounds familiar, there's a good reason why: The Sentinel was apparently based on The Citadel, a military college in Charleston.

329

A living Swamp Fox

South Carolina history buffs know that American Revolutionary War General Francis Marion was nicknamed the "Swamp Fox" for his guerrilla fighting tactics, which included retreating to swamps after quick attacks on the British. But there's also a three-legged coyote that's legendary around the Citadel's campus that's been named the "Swamp Fox." We're not sure if his guerrilla tactics include scavenging for food from plebes, but you can make your guesses.– *AB*

330

Earthquake of 1886 shakes Charleston to its foundations

The largest earthquake in the history of the southeastern United States rocked Charleston on Aug. 31, 1886, leaving more than 100 people dead and hundreds of buildings leveled. Foreshocks were felt 30 miles away in Summerville in the days leading up to the quake, but when the quake hit, it reportedly damaged buildings as far away as Ohio and Alabama. The quake remained a mystery for decades due to the lack of a known underground fault for 60 miles in any direction, but better detection methods recently uncovered a concealed fault along the coastal plains of Virginia and the Carolinas.

331

County has more—and less—racial diversity

Charleston County grew by a third in population to an estimated 411,406 people between 2000 and 2019, according to U.S. Census data. But the growth wasn't even. The white population increased from 62 percent of residents (192,012 people) in 2000 to 286,338 people in 2019, or 69.6 percent of residents. But the numbers of Black residents increased only slightly – from 106,923 people to 108,199 people. Because the numbers didn't grow much while the overall population expanded, the share of Black residents dropped from just over a third of people living in the county to just over a fourth. Meanwhile, the Hispanic population tripled from 7,434 residents in 2000 to 21,393 people, or 5.2 percent by 2019. The Asian population, while under 2 percent of the total, doubled in the two decades to 7,405 people. – *AB*

332

Facade is only thing left of Bennett Rice Mill

From Washington Street behind the Harris Teeter in downtown Charleston, you can see the facade of an old classically-detailed brick industrial building propped up on part of Union Pier Terminal, which is owned by the S.C. Ports Authority. This western facade is all that's left of Bennett Rice Mill, built around 1845 to process rice with steam power. The facility, commissioned by wealthy planter and Gov. Thomas Bennett in 1844, was used until 1911. Later it was converted into a peanut plant as part of the Planters Peanut and Chocolate Co.

Preservationists later fought to save the mill, but Hurricane Donna in 1960 demolished all but the western facade. The Ports Authority built a steel frame to support the remaining facade, which survived Hurricane Hugo in 1989. – *AB*

333

Charleston's Union Station destroyed by fire in 1947

Downtown Charleston had an impressive passenger railroad station at the intersection of East Bay and Columbus streets in the first half of the 20th century. It was part of terminal operations started by the Charleston Union Station Company, which was chartered by the S.C. General Assembly in 1902. Construction started in 1905 and finished two years later. The station burned in 1947. The site later was sold to the S.C. Ports Authority, which continues to use the area today. – *AB*

334

Square dedicated to Washington in 1881

The city of Charleston developed a park in 1818 next to what is now its City Hall. But in 1881, it dedicated the park as Washington Square to honor George Washington and celebrate the 100th anniversary of the famous Yorktown battle in Virginia that ended the Revolutionary War. Five years later, the square became a "tent city" where survivors lived after they lost their homes in the great earthquake of 1886. Through the years, the Square has been home to several monuments including those honoring the Washington Light Infantry, Elizabeth Jackson, mother to President Andrew Jackson; Francis Salvador, the first Jew to serve in the provincial congresses and the first Jew to die in the Revolutionary War; Confederate Gen. P.G.T. Beauregard; poet Henry Timrod; and Washington.– *AB*

335

Ever heard of Lightwood Alley?

Probably not. Today, it's called Zig Zag Alley, one of Charleston's shortest streets that runs north from Atlantic Street between East Bay and Church streets. Featuring a 90-degree turn in its meandering course, the alley was known for a while as Lightwood Alley before it went back to its original name in the 1970s. – *AB*

336

Secrets of Charleston's gardens

There are several features of Charleston gardens that make people flock to see them. Many have water elements that drown out sounds from the streets. Views from streets are often limited to what you can see from gates, in part because masonry walls often enclose house gardens. Other features may include mirrors, arbors, statuary, urns, benches, gates and fencing, which may be made from brick, wrought iron, cast iron or wooden pickets. Charleston gardens also tend to have plants that are of a scale and size that are appropriate for the space, but also may be peppered with fragrant plants, such as tea olives, magnolias, jasmine and roses. Also look for boxwood hedges and brick borders. Charleston gardeners also work hard to make sure there's something in bloom in each of the four seasons. – *AB*

337

2nd oldest Jewish cemetery in U.S. is in Charleston

The Coming Street Cemetery owned by the Kahal Kadosh Beth Elohim (KKBE) congregation in Charleston is the second-oldest Jewish graveyard in the United States with most of the 600 graves dating from 1750 to 1850. "Founded in 1762, the cemetery lies behind high brick walls, parts of which pre-date the American Revolution," according to StLJewishLight.com. "Many Jews buried here fought in the Revolutionary War, Civil War or the War of 1812; the cemetery also holds the graves of the soldiers' families and descendants. A majority of the graves created before the mid-1800s belong to Sephardic families. Prominent family names include DaCosta, Cohen, Moise and Lopez." – *AB*

338

A large portion of *The Notebook* was filmed in Charleston

Much of the movie *The Notebook* takes place in and around Seabrook Island, a town that's one of South Carolina's sea islands about 20 miles southwest of Charleston. None of the filming, however, took place on the island. Boone Hall Plantation in Mount Pleasant served as Allie's summer house. Many scenes, in fact, that were set in Seabrook were filmed in the town of Mount Pleasant or the greater Charleston area. One of the more iconic scenes, the first date of the couple, Noah and Allie, was filmed at the American Theatre on King Street. – *SB*

339

Commuters experience congestion indigestion

Commuters in the Charleston area sat an average of 51 hours in traffic in 2017, a data point that reflects maddening congestion that has become a citizen flashpoint in recent years. Just a dozen years earlier, commutes sat 40 hours in traffic, according to a transportation study. Comparable areas with worse traffic: Nashville, Austin and Seattle.– *AB*

340

Hurricane Hugo is still a reference point for locals

Just as many people remember where they were when President John F. Kennedy was assassinated or when the Berlin Wall came down, Hurricane Hugo's devastating landfall remains a reference point to locals who experienced the Category 4 storm in 1989. Its path of destruction from Charleston County through Charlotte led to 80 deaths and more than $17 billion in damages (2015 dollars). The storm left 750,000 without power and some 56,000 Lowcountry residents homeless. President George H.W. Bush visited the area and signed a $1.1 billion emergency relief bill. – *AB*.

341

Garden & Gun magazine headquartered in Charleston

Garden & Gun is a fun, slick magazine that dubs itself the "Soul of the South." Founded in 2007, it offers scintillating insights about the South's traditions, lore and loves, including the occasional legendary shotgun or a good brown whiskey. With millions of readers in the South and other areas, it's a civilized read that is much different from the 1970s-era, long-gone nightclub with the same name. The disco opened to "give artists and performers [from Spoleto Festival USA] a late-night joint for post-festival revelry, and the spot rattled on in business until late 1981." Four decades later, people in Charleston are *still* talking about the club. – *AB*

342

Back to back tornadoes ravaged downtown in 1938

Five tornadoes swept through the state of South Carolina on Sept. 29, 1938, two of which slammed down into downtown Charleston within 15 minutes of each other, damaging just about everything in their paths. The second of the two twisters devastated the City Market. The tragic aftermath was documented through photographs, creating a collection of 37 total photos, 30 of which were taken by an eyewitness, Ernest Losse. The photos can be viewed in the Historic Charleston Foundation's 1938 Tornado Photograph Collection in the Lowcountry Digital Library. – *SB*

343

The Charleston peninsula used to look a lot different

The Charleston peninsula has grown exponentially over the last few centuries as developers filled in marsh. More than a third of the peninsula that many Charlestonians find familiar is actually man-made land. The city's police station is built on an old garbage dump, for example. To increase the city's footprint, many of the creeks and marshes surrounding the peninsula's high ground were filled in, making way for development, and, as a result, future floodwater. – *SB*

344

Hollywood filmed O entirely in Charleston

O is a modern adaptation of William Shakespeare's *Othello*, a film set in an American high school rather than 16th-century Venice, Italy. Starring Mekhi Phifer, Julia Stiles and Josh Harnett, the film features different styles of music, ranging from rap to opera. It was entirely filmed in Charleston during the spring of 1999, and was intended for release for the following October, but was delayed due to the Columbine High School school tragedy in Colorado and shelved until its release on Aug. 31, 2001. – *SB*

345

Die Hard with a Vengeance features familiar Lowcountry views

In the sequel to the popular *Die Hard* film, Lt. John McClane returned to play a death-defying game to keep a crazed bomber from destroying various locations throughout New York City. But a few notable locations shown on screen in *Die Hard with a Vengeance* were filmed in the Charleston area. Subway station crash scenes were shot in the Bushy Park area of North Charleston, and a geyser scene took place near Summerville, off Interstate 26. Most recognizably, though, is the old Grace Memorial Bridge spanning the Cooper River, used as the set for a scene in which McClane jumps spectacularly with all of Hollywood's flourish onto a container ship. – *SB*

346

Lifetime's "Army Wives" filmed its seven seasons in Charleston

"*Army Wives* was a television drama that featured a group of women living with their spouses and families on an active Army post. While it was Lifetime network's longest-running series, it also was filmed in the Lowcountry. The series began filming in 2006 using the former Charleston Naval Base in North Charleston, Charleston Field on Poston Road, Boone Hall Plantation and more during its run. The show brought in jobs and millions of dollars to local businesses, according to the S.C. Department of Parks, Recreation and Tourism. – *SB*

347

Charleston Green color boasts a post-Civil War origin

According to a local legend, the almost black Charleston Green color featured on doors and shutters today came about after the Civil War when Union troops sent buckets of black paint to the people of Charleston to help in rebuilding the devastated city. The story goes that the colorful people of Charleston, eventual home of Rainbow Row, couldn't bear to see the Holy City painted in government-issued black, so they mixed it with Confederate yellow and a bit of blue-green, resulting in the Charleston Green we see coating front doors today. Another story: Green shutter paint popular in the 19th century degraded into the almost black color. Yet another tale from the Charleston County Public Library says that the shutters of Charleston homes would be painted black, but during the summer, mold would grow on the surface, creating the Charleston Green hue we know today. – *SB*

348

Charleston's motto appears on its seal, and both tell an interesting story

The seal of Charleston, also incorporated into the city's flag, features the name "Carolopolis," which combines the Latin name for "Charles," and the Greek word for "city." The phrase, "Civitatis Regimine Donata," also appears on the seal, roughly translating to "given to the rule of the citizens" in 1783, both honoring the date of the city's incorporation after the American Revolution as well as celebrating the role of self-governance in American society. The city's motto is also memorialized in the city's seal: "Aedes Mores Juraque Curat," which roughly translates to "She Guards Her Temples, Customs and Laws." – *SB*

349

Local newspaper wins 2015 Pulitzer Prize

The *(Charleston) Post and Courier,* the largest daily newspaper in South Carolina, won what many find to be the top award in journalism in 2015 – the Pulitzer Prize for Public Service. It won the prestigious award for a five-part 2014 series on the impact of domestic violence in the Palmetto State. "Their work told the tales of domestic abuse survivors and of the 300 women in the Palmetto State who have been shot, stabbed, strangled, beaten, bludgeoned or burned to death by men during the past decade while legislators did little to quell the bloodshed," according to an article on the prize. The state legislature later passed tougher domestic violence laws. The newspaper also won a Pulitzer Prize in 1925 in editorial writing. – *AB*

350

Charleston City Paper is region's largest alt-weekly

The *Charleston City Paper* hasn't won a Pulitzer Prize...yet. An estimated 100,000 people per week read the Lowcountry's largest alternative weekly. Offering award-winning coverage of major news, food, music and arts, the newspaper got its start in 1997 when formed by Noel Mermer, Blair Barna and Stephanie Barna. Tens of thousands of readers vote annually in the newspaper's Best of Charleston reader awards. In 2019, the newspaper was sold to Georgetown lawyer Ed Bell and columnist Andy Brack, who now serves as publisher. – *AB*

CP

Selected Bibliography

We devoured hundreds of pages of sources to develop this book of facts about Charleston. For full documentation, visit the *Charleston City Paper* (www.CharlestonCityPaper.com/350facts) or the book's website (www.CharlestonFacts.com) Here, however, are some outstanding books and websites that will whet your thirst for more information on the Holy City.

Articles and books

Bass, Jack, and Scott Poole. *The Palmetto State: The Making of Modern South Carolina.* The University of South Carolina Press, 2009.

Bruce, Taylor (ed). *Charleston: Wildsam Field Guide.* Wildsam, 2015.

Edgar, Walter. *South Carolina: A History.* The University of South Carolina Press, 1998.

Edgar, Walter, ed. *The South Carolina Encyclopedia.* The University of South Carolina Press, 2006. You can also find the 2,000+ entries from the book online at: www.SCEncyclopedia.org.

Frazier, Herb; Bernard E. Powers and Marjory Wentworth. *We are Charleston: Tragedy and Triumph at Mother Emanuel.* Thomas Nelson, 2016.

Gergel, Richard. *Unexampled Courage: The Blinding of Sgt. Isaac Woodard and the Awakening of President Harry S. Truman and Judge J. Waties Waring.* Sarah Crichton Books, 2019.

Hillinger, Charles. "Charleston: A City of Historical Firsts," *Los Angeles Times*, Aug. 20, 1989.

Historic Charleston Foundation, ed. *The City of Charleston Tour Guide Training Manual.* City of Charleston, 2011.

Shields, David S. *Southern Provisions: The Creation & Revival of a Cuisine.* Chicago. The University of Chicago Press, 2015. Print.

Print and other media

Charleston Chronicle: http://www.CharlestonChronicle.net

Charleston City Paper: http://www.CharlestonCityPaper.com

Charleston Currents: http://www.CharlestonCurrents.com

Garden & Gun: http://www.GardenandGun.com

The (Charleston) Post and Courier: http://www.PostandCourier.com

Websites

Avery Research Center: *https://avery.cofc.edu/*

Charleston Justice Journey: *https://charlestonjusticejourney.org/*

Charleston Museum: *http://www.CharlestonMuseum.org*

Charleston Time Machine:
https://www.ccpl.org/charleston-time-machine

Explore Charleston: *https://www.charlestoncvb.com/*

Gibbes Museum of Art: *http://www.GibbesMuseum.org*

Historic Charleston Foundation: *https://www.historiccharleston.org/*

Hoppin' John's: *https://www.hoppinjohns.com/*

Lowcountry Digital Library: *https://lcdl.library.cofc.edu/*

Preservation Society of Charleston:
https://www.preservationsociety.org/

"South Carolina History and Genealogy,"
SCIWAY.net: https://www.sciway.net/hist/

Voices: Stories of Change, Charleston, S.C.:
https://www.africanamericancharleston.com/places/

Wikipedia.org

Index

D

E

F

G

R

S

T

www.CharlestonCityPaper.com